LEADERSHIP IN GOD'S KINGDOM

LEADERSHIP IN GOD'S KINGDOM

(Maximising your leadership potential)

REV. MICHAEL KOLA EWUOSHO

ISBN: 978-1-964462-65-3 Paperback
ISBN: 978-1-964462-66-0 Ebook

Rev. date: 07/31/2024

CONTENTS

ACKNOWLEDGMENT

THIS TO ACKNOWLEDGE the roles, contributions of others into my life and ministry hence their contribution in the making of this book.

My wife, Rev. Funke Ewuosho stands out as my partner in life and ministry. Her contributions are incalculable as they stretch beyond human comprehension. Too numerous to count. I thank God for bringing us together in marriage and eventually in ministry.

Our team of pastors who oversee the work of the ministry in the various nations where we have installations are making huge contributions to the development of the ministry and hence the effectiveness in touching more lives around the world. They are hereby acknowledged too.

Our immediate family made up of our adult children, some of whom are married also are acknowledged. Thank you for your contributions, love and understanding as we partner together to fulfil God's purposes for every aspect of life. Thanks.

INTRODUCTION

LEADERSHIP IS THE capacity to influence others through inspiration motivated by a passion, generated by a vision, produced by a conviction, ignited by a purpose.

The creation and blessing of God on mankind shows we were designed to be leaders- discovering and developing our leadership potential is what brings fulfilment in our lives! We see this in God's creation plans.

Genesis 1:26-29

And God said, Let us make man in our image, after our likeness: and let them have dominion over the fish of the sea, and over the fowl of the air, and over the cattle, and over all the earth, and over every creeping thing that creepeth upon the earth. So God created man in his own image, in the image of God created he him; male and female created he them. And God blessed them, and God said unto them, Be fruitful, and multiply, and replenish the earth, and subdue it: and have dominion over the fish of the sea, and over the fowl of the air, and over every living thing that moveth upon the earth.

> *"And God said, Behold, I have given you every herb bearing seed, which is upon the face of all the earth, and every tree, in the which is the fruit of a tree yielding seed; to you it shall be for meat."*

The principle of responsibility and accountability go hand in hand with God's creation plans. How mankind handles the authority given by God goes a long way to affect every other created thing on earth.

Effective Stewardship of all we are given plays a great part in the eventual outcomes of our lives on earth.

I have seen too many people fail, many leaders fall. Its very possible we point fingers at them as if they deliberately planned to fail or fall. We need to know about the right foundations, the process involved in the making of a leader and so many aspects of the development of a leader so we learn how some have aborted the processes and hence the outcomes of their lives that we see. In this book we want to learn what we can as we study the life of Peter, an apostle of Jesus Christ, alongside other leaders, so we can see the foundation laid, the process he went through and how he managed his humanity in the face of the divine assignment he had.

Many fail because they were not aware that being called is not the same as being ready to do the bidding of Him who called. Foundations need to be laid as old ones need to be destroyed or adjusted. Many abort the process of mentoring, serving and growth in service as they throw themselves at tasks they were not prepared for.

There are many facets involved in the making of a leader in God's Kingdom. They include, embracing a Kingdom Vision; Developing Capacity through service; Recognising the human potential for pride; and learning to work with others in Team Work.

CHAPTER 1

Foundations For Leadership

APOSTLE PAUL, in addressing the Corinthian Church, showing their carnality and immaturity by their way of being sectarian, he went on to discuss how he had laboured to lay the foundation of their faith in Christ.

Many are not conscious of any foundation laid in their lives. They just assume that being born again and committing to a church is all that is needed to lay a proper foundation. They assume that growth, or development are guaranteed as long as they go to church and do a few religious things. So when in future they are positioned for leadership in church, they reveal what was in their foundation. Growth and development must be intentional, we need deliberate actions that would result in our growth and eventual maturity in Christ. Our growth can be measured by how much we are being conformed to the image of Christ in character and power.

The Apostle Paul clearly states that the proper Foundation has been laid which is Christ Jesus, but everyone should watch what he builds on that foundation. The Church as a whole is built on the Foundation of Christ as He said in Mathew 16, He is building on the revelation of His Person. But the individual needs to ensure that he or she is built on the right foundation upon which the Church as a whole has been built. If it is possible to build with things different from Christ, it stands to reason that not all have a clear understanding of the right foundation and how to build thereon.

1 Corinthians 3:10-15 (AMP)

10 According to the grace (the special endowment for my task) of God bestowed on me, like a skillful architect and master builder I laid [the] foundation, and now another [man] is building upon it. But let each [man] be careful how he builds upon it,

11 For no other foundation can anyone lay than that which is [already] laid, which is Jesus Christ (the Messiah, the Anointed One). 12 But if anyone builds upon the Foundation, whether it be with gold, silver, precious stones, wood, hay, straw,

13 The work of each [one] will become [plainly, openly] known (shown for what it is); for the day [of Christ] will disclose and declare it, because it will be revealed with fire, and the fire will test and critically appraise the character and worth of the work each person has done.

14 If the work which any person has built on this Foundation [any product of his efforts whatever] survives [this test], he will get his reward.

15 But if any person's work is burned up [under the test], he will suffer the loss [of it all, losing his reward], though he himself will be saved, but only as [one who has passed] through fire.

Jesus Christ is the Foundation upon which the entire church is built. Now individuals need to build the foundations of their lives on Him. Many have built their foundation of their faith on human wisdom, which God calls foolishness in the light of His wisdom. Let us see how Jesus Himself introduces the concept of His building the Church.

Matthew 16:15-19 (AMP)

15 He said to them, But who do you [yourselves] say that I am? 16 Simon Peter replied, You are the Christ, the Son of the living God.

17 Then Jesus answered him, Blessed (happy, fortunate, and to be envied) are you, Simon Bar-Jonah. For flesh and blood [men] have not revealed this to you, but My Father Who is in heaven.

18 And I tell you, you are Peter [Greek, Petros—a large piece of rock], and on this rock [Greek, petra—a huge rock like Gibraltar] I will build

My church, and the gates of Hades (the powers of the infernal region) shall not overpower it [or be strong to its detriment or hold out against it].

19 I will give you the keys of the kingdom of heaven; and whatever you bind (declare to be improper and unlawful) on earth must be what is already bound in heaven; and whatever you loose (declare lawful) on earth must be what is already loosed in heaven.

We see Peter encountering the truth about Jesus and he was told that the encounter was with the Father as He revealed His Son's identity to Peter. This is revelation knowledge. The same thing apostle Paul prayed for the Ephesian church about, in Ephesians chapter 1:17-23. Peter encountered truth that caused a name change for him as Jesus said and upon the rock of the revelation of Christ's identity, He said He will build His Church.

Ephesians 1:17-23 (AMP)

17 [For I always pray to] the God of our Lord Jesus Christ, the Father of glory, that He may grant you a spirit of wisdom and revelation [of insight into mysteries and secrets] in the [deep and intimate] knowledge of Him,

18 By having the eyes of your heart flooded with light, so that you can know and understand the hope to which He has called you, and how rich is His glorious inheritance in the saints (His set-apart ones),

19 And [so that you can know and understand] what is the immeasurable and unlimited and surpassing greatness of His power in and for us who believe, as demonstrated in the working of His mighty strength,

20 Which He exerted in Christ when He raised Him from the dead and seated Him at His [own] right hand in the heavenly [places],

21 Far above all rule and authority and power and dominion and every name that is named [above every title that can be conferred], not only in this age and in this world, but also in the age and the world which are to come.

22 And He has put all things under His feet and has appointed Him the universal and supreme Head of the church [a headship exercised throughout the church],

23 Which is His body, the fullness of Him Who fills all in all [for in that body lives the full measure of Him Who makes everything complete, and Who fills everything everywhere with Himself].

Revelation knowledge is imparted by the Father God so that the knowledge we have had will take on a new dimension in its power to impact us and through us impact others. There are two kinds of knowledge: head knowledge and Heart knowledge. We first know things in our heads through reading, hearing, studying and learning. Then the Father opens our hearts to understand what we had known in our heads before. This creates a high dimension of impact on us as we are granted revealed knowledge. I believe this is the kind of knowledge apostle Paul had as he laboured in the word in the deserts after his miraculous conversion on the way to Damascus.

Back to Peter's story, he had the revelation of Jesus Christ and the Lord said He will build His church on the revelation of who He (Jesus Christ) is. The church Jesus is building has authority on earth to stop the works of the enemy, satan and his cohorts. He also gave the keys of the kingdom of Heaven to the church so that with kingdom authority and power, the Church can bind and loose things on earth as they are available in heaven. What authority, what power! No wonder satan majors on keeping the church ignorant or confused about the truth.

One of the greatest counterfeit that satan has given the church is the religious spirit. This spirit has come to sound like the Holy Spirit and so many people are confused. Religious spirits were involved in keeping the Jews from receiving Jesus Christ as the Son of God. Being built on the foundation of the teachings of Moses, they could not see how the same God will send someone contrary to how they read Moses. That spirit is still around today. The spirit simply accommodates the works of the flesh and puts emphasis on human accomplishments as the basis for anything in God. We can dedicate a whole book to understanding this spirit.

BUILDING ON CHRIST, THE SURE FOUNDATION.

To build on Christ is to build on His person, His labour of love and His assignment from the Father. His death, Burial and Resurrection as well as His ascendance to the Father to sit at His right hand to make intercession for us. God sent His Son, amongst other things to show us who the

Father is, to show us how to live under the authority of the Father and to bring us into the kind of relationship he has with the Father. These He accomplished through His death, burial and resurrection.

Matthew 7:24-27 (NKJV)

Build on the Rock

24 "Therefore whoever hears these sayings of Mine, and does them, I will liken him to a wise man who built his house on the rock: 25 and the rain descended, the floods came, and the winds blew and beat on that house; and it did not fall, for it was founded on the rock.

26 "But everyone who hears these sayings of Mine, and does not do them, will be like a foolish man who built his house on the sand: 27 and the rain descended, the floods came, and the winds blew and beat on that house; and it fell. And great was its fall."

Building on the Word leads to victory in every aspect of our lives. In furtherance of our understanding of building on Christ as the right foundation we need to understand the three dimensions that Christ represents to us as individuals and as leaders in the development process and maximisation of our leadership potential. These are Divine Exchange, then the Divine Pattern, then the Divine Revelation of the love of the Father God.

DIVINE EXCHANGE.

In His death, burial and resurrection, He took our place. This we call "Divine exchange". He took our place so can become as He is. He bore our shame so we can share his glory. He was rejected so we can be accepted in the beloved. He became poor that we through His poverty can be made rich. He bore our sickness and diseases so that by His stripes we are healed.

Isaiah 53:3-8 (AMP)

3 He was despised and rejected and forsaken by men, a Man of sorrows and pains, and acquainted with grief and sickness; and like One from Whom men hide their faces He was despised, and we did not appreciate His worth or have any esteem for Him.

4 Surely He has borne our griefs (sicknesses, weaknesses, and distresses) and carried our sorrows and pains [of punishment], yet we [ignorantly] considered Him stricken, smitten, and afflicted by God [as if with leprosy].

5 But He was wounded for our transgressions, He was bruised for our guilt and iniquities; the chastisement [needful to obtain] peace and well-being for us was upon Him, and with the stripes [that wounded] Him we are healed and made whole.

6 All we like sheep have gone astray, we have turned every one to his own way; and the Lord has made to light upon Him the guilt and iniquity of us all.

7 He was oppressed, [yet when] He was afflicted, He was submissive and opened not His mouth; like a lamb that is led to the slaughter, and as a sheep before her shearers is dumb, so He opened not His mouth.

8 By oppression and judgment He was taken away; and as for His generation, who among them considered that He was cut off out of the land of the living [stricken to His death] for the transgression of my [Isaiah's] people, to whom the stroke was due?

2 Corinthians 5:14-21 (AMP)

14 For the love of Christ controls and urges and impels us, because we are of the opinion and conviction that [if] One died for all, then all died;

15 And He died for all, so that all those who live might live no longer to and for themselves, but to and for Him Who died and was raised again for their sake.

16 Consequently, from now on we estimate and regard no one from a [purely] human point of view [in terms of natural standards of value]. [No] even though we once did estimate Christ from a human viewpoint and as a man, yet now [we have such knowledge of Him that] we know Him no longer [in terms of the flesh].

17 Therefore if any person is [ingrafted] in Christ (the Messiah) he is a new creation (a new creature altogether); the old [previous moral and spiritual condition] has passed away. Behold, the fresh and new has come!

18 But all things are from God, Who through Jesus Christ reconciled us to Himself [received us into favour, brought us into harmony with Himself] and gave to us the ministry of reconciliation [that by word and deed we might aim to bring others into harmony with Him].

19 It was God [personally present] in Christ, reconciling and restoring the world to favor with Himself, not counting up and holding against [men] their trespasses [but cancelling them], and committing to us the message of reconciliation (of the restoration to favor).

20 So we are Christ's ambassadors, God making His appeal as it were through us. We [as Christ's personal representatives] beg you for His sake to lay hold of the divine favor [now offered you] and be reconciled to God.

21 For our sake He made Christ [virtually] to be sin Who knew no sin, so that in and through Him we might become [endued with, viewed as being in, and examples of] the righteousness of God [what we ought to be, approved and acceptable and in right relationship with Him, by His goodness].

In "Divine exchange" He became sin, who knew no sin, that we might become the righteousness of God in Christ. We need to build on this dimension of His sacrifice for us.

THE DIVINE PATTERN

There is another dimension to His death, burial and resurrection and this is what we call the "Divine Pattern". His death, burial and resurrection is the pattern for all to come into maturity. When He told His disciples that they needed to "Deny themselves, Take up their cross" and Follow Him. He had coded His death, burial and resurrection into their pattern for maturity. We can trace this pattern in some of the lives of the old testament saints who served God's purposes in their times. People like Joseph and Moses. Joseph definitely went through the death, burial and resurrection of God's dream for his life.

John 12:24-26 (AMP)

24 I assure you, most solemnly I tell you, Unless a grain of wheat falls into the earth and dies, it remains [just one grain; it never becomes

more but lives] by itself alone. But if it dies, it produces many others and yields a rich harvest.

25 Anyone who loves his life loses it, but anyone who hates his life in this world will keep it to life eternal. [Whoever has no love for, no concern for, no regard for his life here on earth, but despises it, preserves his life forever and ever.]

26 If anyone serves Me, he must continue to follow Me [to cleave steadfastly to Me, conform wholly to My example in living and, if need be, in dying] and wherever I am, there will My servant be also. If anyone serves Me, the Father will honor him.

Matthew 16:24-27 (AMP)

24 Then Jesus said to His disciples, If anyone desires to be My disciple, let him deny himself [disregard, lose sight of, and forget himself and his own interests] and take up his cross and follow Me [cleave steadfastly to Me, conform wholly to My example in living and, if need be, in dying, also].

25 For whoever is bent on saving his [temporal] life [his comfort and security here] shall lose it [eternal life]; and whoever loses his life [his comfort and security here] for My sake shall find it [life everlasting].

26 For what will it profit a man if he gains the whole world and forfeits his life [his blessedlife in the kingdom of God]? Or what would a man give as an exchange for his [blessed]life [in the kingdom of God]?

27 For the Son of Man is going to come in the glory (majesty, splendor) of His Father with His angels, and then He will render account and reward every man in accordance with what he has done.

To build on Christ as the foundation is to love Jesus and be willing to do His word. Thereby we build on the rock and the storms of life will not pull down the house. It is to embrace the will of God and yield to His ways and fulfil His purposes in our lives. It is to re-educate our minds and cultivate the lifestyle that promotes the values of the kingdom of God.

We need to have a new identity, who we are in Christ. We need to recognise the authority we have in the name of Jesus Christ. Then we need to know the process of dying to the things of the flesh, of the world and the things that stir up our lustful desires that can open us up to demonic deceptions. The surest way to allow this process is obedience to God's word, when it is convenient and when it is not.

The seed in John 12, is likened to the word of God in our recreated human spirit. When the seed is sown, the earth and its constituents deal with the shell of the seed such that it disintegrates, then the life in the seed begins to sprout into little plants. The life is in the seed but until it dies, it cannot the release the power of that life. Same with us, there is life in our recreated spirit but until the death process is yielded to, we can not see the full import of the potential God put in us. This rings true in every facet of life. Something dies for something to live. You give up to go up.

A good example of this is the marriage covenant and how to build a successful home under God. The bible says Husbands should love their wives as Christ loved the church and gave Himself for her. Wives are told to submit to their husbands as unto the Lord. The Lord is the centre and model for each person in marriage. He is the example of submission as well as headship. He is the head of the church and He gave His life by laying it down. He died for us all. He is also the example of submission as He lived His life on earth in full submission to the Father God. Wives submit implies dying to somethings and husbands loving as Christ loved implies dying to somethings too. A successful home is a place where both parties are dying and being raised all the time. God raises the dead all the time and the cycle continues.

The 3rd Dimension of Christ's coming to the earth is to show us the Love of God the Father. The fatherhood of God was one of the most difficult for the Jews to comprehend in the days of Jesus on earth. To say you were a son of God puts you in a position like God. For this they planned to kill Him. Many in the church think of love as a feeling. God's love is not based on feelings but on decisions. God's love is a self sacrificing love. It is a giving love. For God so loved that He gave. He gave His only begotten Son, He gave His best for us.

When these dimensions are laid in our lives, we are able to interpret the different dealings in our lives and eventually make the appropriate decisions as we go through the process. We need to recognise our new identity and authority in Christ. We need to cultivate intimacy with God so we know what biblical principle to apply in various stages of our walk with God. There is a time to yield to the process where the flesh dies and we crucify its desires. There is a place where we learn to love as God has loved us. None of these come naturally to us but as we grow in grace, we appreciate these things because we seek to please the Father at all times.

Remember that we have all been predestined to be conformed to the image of Christ. We are to be conformed both in character and power. Jesus Christ is the express image of the Father God according to Hebrews 1:3 and we were originally created in the image and likeness of God.

Romans 8:29-30 (NKJV)

29 For whom He foreknew, He also predestined to be conformed to the image of His Son, that He might be the firstborn among many brethren. 30 Moreover whom He predestined, these He also called; whom He called, these He also justified; and whom He justified, these He also glorified.

Jesus is the author (beginning, foundation,basis, model,) and the finisher (end result, manifestation of the end result, God's glory) of our faith life.

Hebrews 12:1-2 (NKJV)

The Race of Faith

1 Therefore we also, since we are surrounded by so great a cloud of witnesses, let us lay aside every weight, and the sin which so easily ensnares us, and let us run with endurance the race that is set before us, 2 looking unto Jesus, the author and finisher of our faith, who for the joy that was set before Him endured the cross, despising the shame, and has sat down at the right hand of the throne of God.

To be built on Christ our sure foundation is to be built on His word, His character and the different dimensions we have mentioned in this chapter. Knowing how to apply these dimensions needs the help of the Holy Spirit in our lives. God can be counted on to perform His word as He watches over His word to perform it. When we build on His word, He will do His part as we do ours.

Questions to help you reflect on what you have learnt in Chapter 1.

What do you understand by being built on Christ, the solid Rock? How do you see the dimensions of the sacrifices of our Lord Jesus Christ affecting your life?

Letting the Word of God have final authority in your life, implies that you prefer to think, talk and act on the word, over and above your feelings, comfort and initial thoughts. Submitting to the Lordship of Jesus Christ is submitting to the authority of the Word of God. Think on these things. Use your journal to jot your thoughts and share them with friends and colleagues.

CHAPTER 2

Process. (The Adventure of Undergoing Real Changes in Our Lives)

APOSTLE PETER'S LIFE serves as a good example of what it means to go through process. From being introduced to Jesus to having a direct encounter with Him in the "multitude of fish" episode, then having a revelation of who Christ is and going on to denying Him later in the story, we see a man who eventually could say "look on us" then "why look on us" in the book of Acts chapter 3.

Process is what you go through, by choice, when through obedience, yielding to God, you allow the nature of Christ within your spirit to dominate your soul and body. It is supposed to be an ongoing experience as we move from one level of glory to another. It is what you go through when you allow forgiveness rather than retaliation, humility rather than pride. Death works on the flesh and it's tendencies when Life flows from your recreated human spirit.

How did Peter handle the experience of being told, "get behind me, Satan", these words came from Jesus when we read him trying to 'encourage' Jesus not to talk about His death on the cross? Why did he not allow offence to break his fellowship with the Lord?

Matthew 16:21-25 (AMP)

21 From that time forth Jesus began [clearly] to show His disciples that He must go to Jerusalem and suffer many things at the hands of the

elders and the high priests and scribes, and be killed, and on the third day be raised from death.

22 Then Peter took Him aside to speak to Him privately and began to reprove and charge Him sharply, saying, God forbid, Lord! This must never happen to You!

23 But Jesus turned away from Peter and said to him, Get behind Me, Satan! You are in My way [an offence and a hindrance and a snare to Me]; for you are minding what partakes not of the nature and quality of God, but of men.

24 Then Jesus said to His disciples, If anyone desires to be My disciple, let him deny himself [disregard, lose sight of, and forget himself and his own interests] and take up his cross and follow Me [cleave steadfastly to Me, conform wholly to My example in living and, if need be, in dying, also].

25 For whoever is bent on saving his [temporal] life [his comfort and security here] shall lose it [eternal life]; and whoever loses his life [his comfort and security here] for My sake shall find it [life everlasting].

The same Peter, was told by Jesus that he would deny Him.

Matthew 26:31-35 (AMP)

31 Then Jesus said to them, You will all be offended and stumble and fall away because of Me this night [distrusting and deserting Me], for it is written, I will strike the Shepherd, and the sheep of the flock will be scattered.

32 But after I am raised up [to life again], I will go ahead of you to Galilee.

33 Peter declared to Him, Though they all are offended and stumble and fall away because of You [and distrust and desert You], I will never do so.

34 Jesus said to him, Solemnly I declare to you, this very night, before a single rooster crows, you will deny and disown Me three times.

35 Peter said to Him, Even if I must die with You, I will not deny or disown You! And all the disciples said the same thing.

The question is this "was Peter lying?" No he was not lying but was counting on his love for Jesus. His human love failed to stand the test of time when the trial happened. Peter denied Jesus exactly as Jesus had predicted it, three times before the cock crowed. Peter was shattered, he had come to an end of his human love, human ability and strength of human conviction. This is part of process, coming to an end of self. The place of personal development is not so we can depend on self but so we can be at our best when we need to. What a balance this calls for!

We can count on Him who dwells within us when we are born again. The floods will come, the rains will come, it is the house built on the rock that will stand. The man who does the word of God will build the house on the rock and that house will stand. The alternative is to build on sand. The flesh of man was made of the earthly matter. So to build on sand can be seen as to build on humanistic philosophies.

Luke 6:45-49 (AMP)

45 The upright (honorable, intrinsically good) man out of the good treasure [stored] in his heart produces what is upright (honorable and intrinsically good), and the evil man out of the evil storehouse brings forth that which is depraved (wicked and intrinsically evil); for out of the abundance (overflow) of the heart his mouth speaks.

46 Why do you call Me, Lord, Lord, and do not [practice] what I tell you?

47 For everyone who comes to Me and listens to My words [in order to heed their teaching] and does them, I will show you what he is like:

48 He is like a man building a house, who dug and went down deep and laid a foundation upon the rock; and when a flood arose, the torrent broke against that house and could not shake or move it, because it had been securely built orfounded on a rock.

49 But he who merely hears and does not practice doing My words is like a man who built a house on the ground without a foundation, against which the torrent burst, and immediately it collapsed and fell, and the breaking and ruin of that house was great.

The tests came for Peter and he failed but by the third chapter of the book of Acts, the same Peter had come to terms with building on the rock not on sand anymore.

Acts 3:6-12 (AMP)

6 But Peter said, Silver and gold (money) I do not have; but what I do have, that I give to you: in [theuse of] the name of Jesus Christ of Nazareth, walk!

7 Then he took hold of the man's right hand with a firm grip and raised him up. And at once his feet and ankle bones became strong and steady,

8 And leaping forth he stood and began to walk, and he went into the temple with them, walking and leaping and praising God.

9 And all the people saw him walking about and praising God,

10 And they recognised him as the man who usually sat [begging] for alms at the Beautiful Gate of the temple; and they were filled with wonder and amazement (bewilderment, consternation) over what had occurred to him.

11 Now while he [still] firmly clung to Peter and John, all the people in utmost amazement ran together and crowded around them in the covered porch (walk) called Solomon's.

12 And Peter, seeing it, answered the people, You men of Israel, why are you so surprised and wondering at this? Why do you keep staring at us, as though by our [own individual] power or [active] piety we had made this man [able] to walk?

Acts 3:13-16 (NKJV)

13 The God of Abraham, Isaac, and Jacob, the God of our fathers, glorified His Servant Jesus, whom you delivered up and denied in the presence of Pilate, when he was determined to let Him go. 14 But you denied the Holy One and the Just, and asked for a murderer to be granted to you, 15 and killed the Prince of life, whom God raised from the dead, of which we are witnesses. 16 And His name, through faith in His name, has made this man strong, whom you see and know.

Yes, the faith which comes through Him has given him this perfect soundness in the presence of you all.

He spoke to the man, pulled him up and yet gave the credit to faith in the name of Jesus. This is what process does in a man who allows himself to be processed in the things pertaining to God's kingdom. He did not yield to offence when he was told "get thee behind Me". He did not allow his sense of failure completely discourage him from following after Jesus and His demands of the kingdom of God. He still bounced back in faith and humbly gave the credit to the name of Jesus Christ for the healing of the man in the book of Acts, chapter 3. Thank God for the intercession of Jesus Christ for Peter. Well, He is presently at the right side of the Father- God, making intercession for us today!

UNDERSTANDING OUR PROGRAMMING. (WE HAVE BEEN PROGRAMMED BY OUR NATURE, NURTURE AND CULTURE.)

Luke 6:46

Why do you call Me, Lord, Lord, and do not [practice] what I tell you?

In Luke 6, Our Lord Jesus asked a question, when he was physically on earth, and that question still needs to be answered in our context today. The question was " why do you call me Lord, Lord and do not the things which I say?" The question, amongst other things, challenges our understanding and application of His Lordship over us, as well as our recognition of the fact that His Word should have authority over our lives. In our present day world all these have a place in our study and thoughts, but I think an answer today will be " Lord, the things that inform what we do have been established in us before we accepted you as our Lord so we have no place for what you say. Moreover, what you say runs contrary to what we have been programmed to do and how we live our lives". "By our old nature (inherited from Adam) we are not designed to 'love our enemies' or 'bless those who curse us'.

The new birth starts with the injection of God's life (Zoe in Greek) into our spirits. When we receive Jesus as our Lord and Saviour having repented of our sins, we have our human spirits recreated by the Holy Spirit infusing God's life into us. We now have a new identity–in Christ.

We become a part of the new creation, with Jesus Christ as the head of this new creation replacing Adam as the failed head of the old creation. This life is in our spirits but the inherited nature we had is still lodged in our souls (our minds, will and emotions). James 1:21 tells us to lay aside naughtiness, amongst other things in our souls, and receive, with meekness the engrafted word, which is able to save our souls. Work needs to be done in our souls so we can come into alignment with the way God ordained for things to function in our lives on the earth. Our souls (the seat of our personality) have been affected by the sinfulness in our world, our old nature and the our experiences before we met Christ. Without the development of our spirits in the life of God, we can still live as people who are governed by the dictates of the human flesh and not yield to the Spirit of God who lives within us. The Corinthian church, in the days of Apostle Paul were full of the manifestations of the Spirit in gifts yet they were ruled by their flesh according to 1Cor. 3.

God's Word is designed to train us to walk in the victory that has been granted us through the death, burial and resurrection of our Lord Jesus Christ. Many Christians are not taking full advantage of their privileges in Christ. God raised Paul to help bring us all into the fullness of what we have become -in Christ.

UNDERSTAND HOW WE GET OUR PROGRAMMING.

We all get programmed in our souls through 'observation, imitation and repetition '. The advertising companies know this and are taking full advantage of it. Even a relaxed observation when it is repeated can influence us. Our nature, (inherited nature from Adam and our temperaments), our nurture (how we were brought up) and culture (the environment in which we have grown) have been known to define who we are and inform what we do and how we go about things. Our culture is a body of accepted norms, traditions, practises and generally inform our environment. Our nurture is how we were brought up: in love and acceptance, in discipline or tyranny, to love development or cultivate self destructive habits. Our nature has to do with our inherited nature from Adam, as well as our inborn temperament and general human tendencies. Each person is pretty much defined by these. Satan, the god of this world, on the other hand has our carnal mind, the worldly systems and his cohorts of evil spirits to enhance his operations in our lives. He has come to steal, kill and destroy. Some of the time, it seems he is not the one to deal with directly but the influence of the culture in which we live.

LESSONS FROM THE PRODIGAL SON AND PARABLE OF THE SOWER.

The story of the prodigal son shows the influence of the environment or culture that the son allowed into his life. The thought that receiving his inheritance immediately will give him the freedom to enjoy his life without the regulation of the father came from the culture in which he grew. It's happening today, "why wait till you are married before enjoying sex?" do it now! Get it all now! Such thinking does not help people see far enough for the consequences that follow such. This story shows one of such. The devil seems not to be in the picture at all. The environment, prevailing thought patterns and culture informed his way of life, desires, expectations and hence experience. Thank God for a loving Father who can accept us in spite of our foolishness. See Luke 15:11-32.

Luke 15:11-24 (NKJV)

The Parable of the Lost Son

11 Then He said: "A certain man had two sons. 12 And the younger of them said to his father, 'Father, give me the portion of goods that falls to me.' So he divided to them his livelihood. 13 And not many days after, the younger son gathered all together, journeyed to a far country, and there wasted his possessions with prodigal living. 14 But when he had spent all, there arose a severe famine in that land, and he began to be in want. 15 Then he went and joined himself to a citizen of that country, and he sent him into his fields to feed swine. 16 And he would gladly have filled his stomach with the pods that the swine ate, and no one gave him anything.

17 "But when he came to himself, he said, 'How many of my father's hired servants have bread enough and to spare, and I perish with hunger! 18 I will arise and go to my father, and will say to him, "Father, I have sinned against heaven and before you, 19 and I am no longer worthy to be called your son. Make me like one of your hired servants."'

20 "And he arose and came to his father. But when he was still a great way off, his father saw him and had compassion, and ran and fell on his neck and kissed him. 21 And the son said to him, 'Father, I have sinned against heaven and in your sight, and am no longer worthy to be called your son.'

22 "But the father said to his servants, 'Bring out the best robe and put it on him, and put a ring on his hand and sandals on his feet. 23 And bring the fatted calf here and kill it, and let us eat and be merry; 24 for this my son was dead and is alive again; he was lost and is found.' And they began to be merry.

"When he came to himself " is when he repented, had a change of mind and was willing to renounce his thoughts and actions and return to a healthy relationship with his father. The source of those derailing thoughts was Satan, the avenues through which they came to him were his environment that have influenced his thought processes through his humanity. Pride is one quality that prevails in our human thoughts and tendencies.

The Parable of the sower.

Mark 4:14-20 (AMP)

14 The sower sows the Word.

15 The ones along the path are those who have the Word sown [in their hearts], but when they hear, Satan comes at once and [by force] takes away the message which is sown in them.

16 And in the same way the ones sown upon stony ground are those who, when they hear the Word, at once receive and accept and welcome it with joy;

17 And they have no real root in themselves, and so they endure for a little while; then when trouble or persecution arises on account of the Word, they immediately are offended (become displeased, indignant, resentful) and they stumble and fall away.

18 And the ones sown among the thorns are others who hear the Word;

19 Then the cares and anxieties of the world and distractions of the age, and the pleasure and delight and false glamour and deceitfulness of riches, and the craving and passionate desire for other things creep in and choke and suffocate the Word, and it becomes fruitless.

20 And those sown on the good (well-adapted) soil are the ones who hear the Word and receive and accept and welcome it and bear fruit—some thirty times as much as was sown, some sixty times as much, and some [even] a hundred times as much.

In the parable of the sower, we see the enemy mentioned in only one case of the seed being stolen for their lack of paying attention to the word they heard. Satan is said to be the direct cause for this unproductive soil (heart) of the four examples given for the types of soil that determined the productivity of the seed. In the stony ground and the thorny one we see the culture once again affecting the heart, hence the soil. The stony heart received the word with gladness but have no root in themselves, no time to develop a root system of understanding. The persecution or tribulation comes directly from either the devil, the environment or from wrong expectations from within. In the thorny heart, the cares,the deceitfulness of riches and desires for other things, all come from culture and nurture. Satan is behind all these but we are learning what his channels are in getting the word to be unproductive in the lives of people. From the book of Mark 4:13-20 We see these things clearly.

We need to take responsibility for our future. This sense of responsibility will help us stop allowing excuses in our lives. Failure has a lot of excuses and success does not need any explanation. So decide to be a success with God. The decision to be a success in God is the reason why we can challenge our thoughts and examine our ways. Things only change when we decide to change.

We need to Examine the philosophy at work in each person. Our inner philosophy will determine or influence the quality of decisions we make. Apostle John said he was glad when he heard that his people walk in the truth as the truth is in them.

3 John 2-4.

2 Beloved, I pray that all may go well with you and that you may be in good health, as it goes well with your soul.

3 For I rejoiced greatly when the brothers came and testified to your truth, as indeed you are walking in the truth.

4 I have no greater joy than to hear that my children are walking in the truth.

Our lives are greatly determined by our decisions and our decisions are based on the accuracy of knowledge we have. No wonder the same Apostle had earlier said " I wish above all things that you prosper and be in health even as your soul prospers." (3john2). Soul prosperity leads to material prosperity and health. The soul of a human being comprises of the mind, will and emotions. All these are affected by the programming we have all received through our nature, nurture and culture.

For many the process of changing begins when we can have the courage to ask why we think, say and do the things we do, the way we think, say and do them. The answers to these questions will reveal the internal programming at work in us. When God's reality (truth) is not in us then lies have found their way into us. Satan's greatest access into the human race is by injecting thoughts into the mind. The grafting of truth into us as we humbly receive the truth is what will save our souls from all the junk we have imbibed into our minds, emotions and will. All through our growing up days, we have all imbibed many things that are not based on the truth of God's word.

See James 1:21

So get rid of all uncleanness and the rampant outgrowth of wickedness, and in a humble (gentle, modest) spirit receive and welcome the Word which implanted and rooted [in your hearts] contains the power to save your souls. (Amplified bible)

Matthew 15:19

For out of the heart come evil thoughts (reasonings and disputings and designs) such as murder, adultery, sexual vice, theft, false witnessing, slander, and irreverent speech. (Amp. Bible)

If thoughts are not examined, their source may never be identified, hence these thoughts may continue to influence us. These thoughts can influence an entire generation not just an individual. Many even suffer bitter experiences and yet never stop to ponder on the thoughts that led to the experience. Experience analysed is the way to derive lessons and knowledge from the experience itself. Experience is not the best teacher but analysed experience can be.

Our programming may have been filled with poverty, rejection, selfishness and pride. These all came through our nature, nurture and culture. Our motives, focus and intentions should also be examined in the light of God's Word.

Joshua 1:8, psalms 1:1-3 are instructions designed to reprogram ourselves and our lives with God's truth in His Word.

Joshua 1:8

This Book of the Law shall not depart out of your mouth, but you shall meditate on it day and night, that you may observe and do according to all that is written in it. For then you shall make your way prosperous, and then you shall deal wisely and have good success.

Psalms 1:1-3

BLESSED (HAPPY, fortunate, prosperous, and enviable) is the man who walks and lives not in the counsel of the ungodly [following their advice, their plans and purposes], nor stands [submissive and inactive] in the path where sinners walk, nor sits down [to relax and rest] where the scornful [and the mockers] gather.

2 But his delight and desire are in the law of the Lord, and on His law (the precepts, the instructions, the teachings of God) he habitually meditates (ponders and studies) by day and by night.

3 And he shall be like a tree firmly planted [and tended] by the streams of water, ready to bring forth its fruit in its season; its leaf also shall not fade or wither; and everything he does shall prosper [and come to maturity].

It is the meditation, speaking and acting on God's word that begins the process of reprogramming amongst other things in our lives.

STEPS TO REPROGRAMMING.

1. Have the attitude of a winner not a loser.

Your attitude is a function of your knowledge, thoughts and expectations in life. Paul said he has learned to abase and abound and can do all things through Christ who strengthens him. His attitude was, 'no matter my financial state, I will not let the natural control me. I am regulated internally by the presence of the Greater one in me'. A winning attitude seeks to develop, improve and be the best one can be in life.

Practise daily times in worship, meditation and confession of God's word. We challenge contrary thoughts and speak to mountains of doubt, unbelief, un-forgiveness, strife and bitterness or offences.

2. Get rooted in your identity in Christ, by speaking what God says about you and Acting like it is true as you form new habits. Build your expectations on the word of God.

Cast all cares on the Lord and regulate your thoughts through out the day.

Philippians 4:6-8 (AMP)

6 Do not fret or have any anxiety about anything, but in every circumstance and in everything, by prayer and petition (definite requests), with thanksgiving, continue to make your wants known to God.

7 And God's peace [shall be yours, that tranquil state of a soul assured of its salvation through Christ, and so fearing nothing from God and being content with its earthly lot of whatever sort that is, that peace] which transcends all understanding shall garrison and mount guard over your hearts and minds in Christ Jesus.

8 For the rest, brethren, whatever is true, whatever is worthy of reverence and is honorable and seemly, whatever is just, whatever is pure, whatever is lovely and lovable, whatever is kind and winsome and gracious, if there is any virtue and excellence, if there is anything worthy of praise, think on and weigh and take account of these things [fix your minds on them].

3. Set goals for your spiritual, financial, emotional and physical health. Make plans for these to come to pass based on God's word and strategy. Set goals that can help deepen your walk with God. Faith goals as well as natural goals.

Cultivate healthy relationships with people who add value to your life and who can help you become all that God planned for you to be.

Know the Word as seed for all you need. Let the word never depart from your eyes.

Proverbs 4:20-27 (AMP)

20 My son, attend to my words; consent and submit to my sayings.

21 Let them not depart from your sight; keep them in the center of your heart.

22 For they are life to those who find them, healing and health to all their flesh.

23 Keep and guard your heart with all vigilance and above all that you guard, for out of it flow the springs of life.

24 Put away from you false and dishonest speech, and willful and contrary talk put far from you.

25 Let your eyes look right on [with fixed purpose], and let your gaze be straight before you.

26 Consider well the path of your feet, and let all your ways be established and ordered aright.

27 Turn not aside to the right hand or to the left; remove your foot from evil.

Reflecting on insights from chapter 2.

How much of programming do you perceive in your soul? How do you plan to reprogram your life in the light of God's word? Can you see your life reflecting more and more of Christ Jesus as you work on reprogramming your life?

CHAPTER 3

Personal Development

T O BECOME ALL that God planned for you, the subject of personal development is crucial to human existence. It is a subject that has been left out of the christian thoughts and process in many parts of the world. Many success literature have simply taken the principles of the bible and put God out of the philosophy and applied them to human lives and got some results. Whether we think leadership, spirituality, success in life and business, or whatever the area we are considering, the subject of personal development has a crucial role to play. In Leadership, we cannot take people where we have not been. If the leader is not showing an example or leading by example, what will the followers have to model after? When we read that Jesus grew in wisdom, stature and in favour with God and man, it means He grew up all round: mentally, physically, spiritually and socially. Growth does not just happen, it has to be intentional. Many assume that certain activities will produce growth like children who just live their lives and see themselves growing. Others have no concept of growth at all, they just remain the way they have been. Growth activities have to be planned and executed repeatedly and deliberately. To grow up in any area starts by recognising the needs in that area. What do you want to be, to do, to have and where do you want to go? What will it cost to get the results you want. So the first thing is to have a Vision. What are the possibilities that lie around you or in you? With a Vision you then need to map out goals that will bring the fulfilment of the vision. Then the time you want to see the vision accomplished.

The subject generally covered in Personal development and living successfully in all areas of life include 1. Vision, 2. Goal setting, 3. Time Management, 4. Planning and Execution. Then we see the need to learn the following: Leadership Development, Team work, Develop Thinking, Listening and Reading Skills, Developing Communication Skills, and Relationship Building.

We see Jesus in Luke 2:51-52. He grew in these areas.

"And He went down with them and came to Nazareth and was [habitually] obedient to them; and his mother kept and closely and persistently guarded all these things in her heart.

And Jesus increased in wisdom (in broad and full understanding) and in stature and years, and in favor with God and man."

Understanding Goal Setting as part of Personal developmental skills.

(Man here refers to mankind, both male and female.) Man is a spirit, he has a soul and lives in a body. Every aspect of his being is loaded with potential. The various aspects of his being were designed to operate and be governed by God's laws. The three aspects of man's being also interface with one another. There are laws and practises that govern the spiritual, soul dimensions : (Made of the mind, will and emotions) or mental and the physical side of things. To be fully maximised, man needs to develop in all ramifications, engaging the laws and the disciplines needed while going on with his life. He also has other aspects like the socials, where he has to deal with relationships, then he needs to understand the financial aspects of life then he needs to know about his career or calling; his roles in leadership and a heart of serving God's purposes in the lives of people he interacts with. All potential needs discovery, development and eventual deployment. Personal development is designed to develop potential as well as engaging in the disciplines to be productive in all aspects of the life of man.

UNDERSTANDING POTENTIAL.

Every aspect of man, as mentioned earlier is loaded with potential. In the physical realm, we see that our human muscles have the ability to be developed for us to become champions in athletics or any sports. The lazy man has as many muscles as the olympic champion. The difference is in the fact that the champion has harnessed the potential in his physical body through training so that the muscles function as such peak levels of performance to win medals in competitions.

Similar arguments can be made concerning the mind, and relationships or any skill that can be developed through training as well. Same can be said about the spiritual side of life as well. Everything has the potential to increase and be greater and better than the original state in creation. Trees were created but what we use wood to make today go from tables to beds and so many wood based items. With polishing and treatments, raw wood has been designed to become highly utilised items in homes, offices etc. So we were created into an environment where all things with potential await our understanding and application of certain disciplines to become productive in life and very successful. The joy of successful living is in the realisation of developed potential in all areas of our lives.

UNDERSTANDING GOD'S LAWS FOR PRODUCTIVITY

Luke 6:45

The upright (honorable, intrinsically good) man out of the good treasure [stored] in his heart produces what is upright (honorable and intrinsically good), and the evil man out of the evil storehouse brings forth that which is depraved (wicked and intrinsically evil); for out of the abundance (overflow) of the heart his mouth speaks.

The heart of man is a major productive centre for his life and he determines what he stores there and so determines what is released into his life, through his spoken words. So man is responsible for what he stores and what he speaks. They are connected so the heart and mouth connection is a major factor in the spiritual development of man.

Proverbs 4:20-27

20 My son, attend to my words; consent and submit to my sayings.

21 Let them not depart from your sight; keep them in the center of your heart.

22 For they are life to those who find them, healing and health to all their flesh.

23 Keep and guard your heart with all vigilance and above all that you guard, for out of it flow the springs of life.

24 Put away from you false and dishonest speech, and willful and contrary talk put far from you.

25 Let your eyes look right on [with fixed purpose], and let your gaze be straight before you.

26 Consider well the path of your feet, and let all your ways be established and ordered aright.

27 Turn not aside to the right hand or to the left; remove your foot from evil.

God's Word is His major tool for productivity in our lives. We also have a part to play in how we build our relationship with His word. Then how we protect our hearts from other things includes our speech, our ways and our lifestyle in general.

As creatures with the power of choice, we can choose our thoughts, words and actions and all these will impact our productivity in life.

POWER OF WORDS.

Proverbs 18:21 (AMP)

21 Death and life are in the power of the tongue, and they who indulge in it shall eat the fruit of it [for death or life].

Proverbs 13:2-3 (AMP)

A good man eats good from the fruit of his mouth, but the desire of the treacherous is for violence.

He who guards his mouth keeps his life, but he who opens wide his lips comes to ruin.

Mark 11:23-24 (AMP)

Truly I tell you, whoever says to this mountain, Be lifted up and thrown into the sea! and does not doubt at all in his heart but believes that what he says will take place, it will be done for him.

For this reason I am telling you, whatever you ask for in prayer, believe (trust and be confident) that it is granted to you, and you will [get it].

THINKING THOUGHTS.

Proverbs 23:7 (AMP)

For as he thinks in his heart, so is he. As one who reckons, he says to you, eat and drink, yet his heart is not with you [but is grudging the cost].

MEDITATION.

Psalms 1:1-3 (AMP)

BLESSED (HAPPY, fortunate, prosperous, and enviable) is the man who walks and lives not in the counsel of the ungodly [following their advice, their plans and purposes], nor stands [submissive and inactive] in the path where sinners walk, nor sits down [to relax and rest] where the scornful [and the mockers] gather.

But his delight and desire are in the law of the Lord, and on His law (the precepts, the instructions, the teachings of God) he habitually meditates (ponders and studies) by day and by night.

And he shall be like a tree firmly planted [and tended] by the streams of water, ready to bring forth its fruit in its season; its leaf also shall not fade or wither; and everything he does shall prosper [and come to maturity].

Joshua 1:8 (AMP)

This Book of the Law shall not depart out of your mouth, but you shall meditate on it day and night, that you may observe and do according to all that is written in it. For then you shall make your way prosperous, and then you shall deal wisely and have good success.

DILIGENCE (WORKING SMARTER AND HARD WORK)

Proverbs 10:4-5 (AMP)

He becomes poor who works with a slack and idle hand, but the hand of the diligent makes rich.

He who gathers in summer is a wise son, but he who sleeps in harvest is a son who causes shame.

Proverbs 12:24-27 (AMP)

The hand of the diligent will rule, but the slothful will be put to forced labor.

Anxiety in a man's heart weighs it down, but an encouraging word makes it glad.

The [consistently] righteous man is a guide to his neighbor, but the way of the wicked causes others to go astray.

The slothful man does not catch his game or roast it once he kills it, but the diligent man gets precious possessions.

Proverbs 18:9 (AMP)

He who is loose and slack in his work is brother to him who is a destroyer andhe who does not use his endeavors to heal himself is brother to him who commits suicide.

IMAGINATION IS POWERFUL.

Genesis 11:6 (AMP)

And the Lord said, Behold, they are one people and they have all one language; and this is only the beginning of what they will do, and now nothing they have imagined they can do will be impossible for them.

CULTIVATING A PRODUCTIVE LIFE.

A productive life is a life that experiences desired results in all areas of life. We all have desires and our desires will not fall on us like ripe mangoes. They happen as we work towards them. Life seems to have a price tag for every good thing. There is a price to pay and a position to take if we are going to enjoy privileges in life. Success is defined as obtaining desired results. Some one said the only time success comes before work is in the dictionary. In life the work comes before the success.

How do you harness all your faculties and acquire a level of discipline so you can engage yourself in the pursuit of success in any desired area of your life? Your thoughts, words and actions must come into alignment for productivity to be enhanced. It starts with your self image. How do you see yourself? Do you see yourself as capable or otherwise? We may need to work on a healthy self image before any meaningful progress can be made. Since success is defined as achieving desired results, what it takes to achieve the results is what diligence, determination and decisiveness can produce in us. Knowing what to do, being willing to pay the price and then getting down to planning and executing the activities are all involved in having a productive life.

UNDERSTAND HOW GOAL SETTING WORKS.

Goals are objectives or results we want to see or have. They are end results we aim to accomplish. To set them ahead of accomplishing them is what this skill is about. Doing this helps to direct our energies, focus our minds and channel our activities towards accomplishments. The other side of this skill is what we are becoming for accomplishing these goals.

Steps in Goal setting: 1. You must have a specific goal; 2. You must have a specific time you in which to achieve your goal. 3. You must write down your goal. 4. You must develop a plan to achieve your goal. 5. You must decide the price you are willing to pay.. 6. You must think about your goal every day.

Goals need to be set in all areas of life. Your spiritual, financial, relational and career goals need to be set. Goal setting is a necessary skill if our lives will be productive. It also helps us manage our time well. Time management is another skill we need to develop.

CULTIVATING PERSONAL DEVELOPMENT

Vision: your personal vision should encompass your talents, gifts and the discovery, development and deployment of your gifts to meet the needs of others and fulfil your God given dreams.

Personal Development: self awareness should precede personal development programs. If you are unaware of your temperament, the effect of your nurture and environment on your choices and lifestyle, you may not really appreciate the need to set clear goals adapted to suit your individual make up or develop life and time management habits that are peculiar to your aspirations.

Relationships: the ability to cultivate healthy relationships and create a nurturing environment where people can be helped and encouraged to grow and develop their potentials.

Attitude: this is a function of your thoughts and expectation and actions. Wrong thoughts produce wrong actions and these lead to wrong results. So we need to predetermine our anticipated outcomes then generate the right attitudes.

The basic areas where we need to develop can be classified into the following:

Goal setting; Time management; Communication; Leadership development; Understanding how to collaborate with others to build teams. The team makes the dream work.

The Wheel of Life

There are 7 categories we can see to begin to apply ourselves to, namely: physical, Family, Mental, Financial, spiritual, career and personal. We can face these categories individually and first of all have an assessment of where we are in them, grading ourselves from 1-10, 10 being the best and 1 being the least.

Physical : we can look at appearance; regular check up; energy level; muscles toned; regular fitness program, weight control, diet and nutrition, stress control, endurance and strength and others.

Spiritual: our belief in God; inner peace; influence on others, spouse relationship, church involvement, sense of purpose, attitude for giving donations, prayer, bible study and others like evangelism.

Mental: attitude, intelligence, formal education, continuing education and training creative imagination inspirational reading CD education, inquisitive mind, self image, enthusiasm,others.

Family: listening, good role model, principled but flexible, forgiving attitude, building self-esteem of others, express love and respect, meals together, family relationships, dealing with disagreements, time together and others.

7 steps to goal setting

1. Identify the goal
2. List the benefits: what's in it for me?
3. List the obstacles to overcome. You can ask a friend who knows you well to help you on this one.
4. List the skills and knowledge required.

5. Identify the people and groups to work with.
6. Develop a plan of action.
7. Set a deadline for achievement .

Goal setting is about becoming. What you become to accomplish your goals is the key in setting them.

REFLECTING ON INSIGHTS from chapter 3.

Are you ready for full on personal development? What goals are you going to set to fulfil your desired results in various aspects of your life? What are the obstacles that can stop you? What are you going to do about these obstacles?

CHAPTER 4

Understanding Biblical Stewardship

STEWARDSHIP IN CHRISTIANITY follows from the belief that human beings are created by the same God who created the entire universe and everything in it. To look after the Earth, and thus God's dominion, is the responsibility of the **Christian** steward.

Stewardship means the management or care of something, particularly the kind that works. If your company is making money, there's probably been careful **stewardship.**

A **biblical** world view of **stewardship** can be consciously **defined** as: "Utilizing and managing all resources God provides for the glory of God and the betterment of His creation."

Stewards use what is given to serve the purpose of the Giver! What we do as stewards should reflect our knowledge of how things work and how the Giver intends for us to use them to fulfil His purposes!

1 Peter 4:10-11

As each of you has received a gift (a particular spiritual talent, a gracious divine endowment), employ it for one another as [befits] good trustees of God's many-sided grace [faithful stewards of the extremely diverse powers and gifts granted to Christians by unmerited favor].

Whoever speaks, [let him do it as one who utters] oracles of God; whoever renders service, [let him do it] as with the strength which God furnishes abundantly, so that in all things God may be glorified through Jesus Christ (the Messiah). To Him be the glory and dominion forever and ever (through endless ages). Amen (so be it).

1 Corinthians 4:1-2

1 SO THEN, let us [apostles] be looked upon as ministering servants of Christ and stewards (trustees) of the mysteries (the secret purposes) of God.

2 Moreover, it is [essentially] required of stewards that a man should be found faithful [proving himself worthy of trust].

The Bishop or Overseer is God's steward.

Titus 1:7-9 (AMP)

7 For the bishop (an overseer) as God's steward must be blameless, not self-willed or arrogant or presumptuous; he must not be quick-tempered or given to drink or pugnacious (brawling, violent); he must not be grasping and greedy for filthy lucre (financial gain);

8 But he must be hospitable (loving and a friend to believers, especially to strangers and foreigners); [he must be] a lover of goodness [of good people and good things], sober-minded (sensible, discreet), upright and fair-minded, a devout man and religiously correct, temperate and keeping himself in hand.

9 He must hold fast to the sure and trustworthy Word of God as he was taught it, so that he may be able both to give stimulating instruction and encouragement in sound (wholesome) doctrine and to refute and convict those who contradict and oppose it [showing the wayward their error].

General Application of biblical Stewardship.

Everything we have comes from God. James 1:17 says all good and perfect gifts come from Him. He gave them for a purpose. We need to discover His purposes for His gifts.

Everything He gave us has potential to increase, develop, reproduce and become greater than how it was given. How we manage or steward these things will determine how they turn out!

He gives grace to those who acknowledge their dependence on Him. Faith is participating with God for His will, plan and purposes to be fulfilled on earth.

We need to be faithful stewards of all God gives us! Well done good and faithful servant!!!

Our giving, praying and fasting are activities we engage in as we steward our relationship with God. As faithful stewards our motives and focus matter to God. He makes sure we are rewarded.

(See Mathew 6 1-18)

We are to steward His presence, power and character, and how we do these stewardship and discipline will determine how much of all these that are needed in meeting the various needs in our lives and in the lives of others around us will be readily available to us. These become more available to us as we learn to do these things (giving, praying and fasting) with the right motives. He is introducing us to a higher way of living!

He also wants us to lay up treasures in heaven.

Matthew 6:19-24 (AMP)

19 Do not gather and heap up and store up for yourselves treasures on earth, where moth and rust and worm consume and destroy, and where thieves break through and steal.

20 But gather and heap up and store for yourselves treasures in heaven, where neither moth nor rust nor worm consume and destroy, and where thieves do not break through and steal;

21 For where your treasure is, there will your heart be also.

22 The eye is the lamp of the body. So if your eye is sound, your entire body will be full of light.

23 But if your eye is unsound, your whole body will be full of darkness. If then the very light in you [your conscience] is darkened, how dense is that darkness!

24 No one can serve two masters; for either he will hate the one and love the other, or he will stand by and be devoted to the one and despise and beagainst the other. You cannot serve God and mammon (deceitful riches, money, possessions, orwhatever is trusted in).

Faithful in little is faithful in much.

Luke 16:10-13 (AMP)

10 He who is faithful in a very little [thing] is faithful also in much, and he who is dishonest and unjust in a very little [thing] is dishonest and unjust also in much.

11 Therefore if you have not been faithful in the [case of] unrighteous mammon (deceitful riches, money, possessions), who will entrust to you the true riches?

12 And if you have not proved faithful in that which belongs to another [whether God or man], who will give you that which is your own [that is, the true riches]?

13 No servant is able to serve two masters; for either he will hate the one and love the other, or he will stand by and be devoted to the one and despise the other. You cannot serve God and mammon (riches, or anything in which you trust and on which you rely).

Stewardship: Principles of Life Management

1. Everything we have was given to us (by God). James 1:17-25.

2. Everything we are given has potential in them. They can increase, multiply and become greater than how we were given. Think about it. Everything God created has built-in potential. Even the trees in the forest can be made into fine furniture! Greatness is locked into a new born baby. Your mind, muscles and every faculty has the potential to be and do more than it is doing now. We all have 24 hours daily, how we steward our time determines outcomes in our lives.

3. How we handle these things given to us will determine how we are rewarded or judged. Our ability to manage (steward) these things is the key to our success in life.

4. We shall give account to our Giver (God) for how we related, treated and utilized what we were given.

1 Corinthians 4:1-2

Stewards of the Mysteries of God

Let a man so consider us, as servants of Christ and stewards of the mysteries of God. Moreover it is required in stewards that one be found faithful.

5. Our respect for God (fear of God) will determine how we treat His gifts in our lives. His gifts are designed to bless many others, bring fulfillment in our lives, and bring satisfaction to His heart (glory to God). (Proverbs 22:4) by humility and the fear of The Lord are riches and honour and life.

6. The purpose of anything is usually in the mind of the Maker (God). When purpose is not known, abuse is inevitable. When things given are abused, their potential remain untapped and the benefits derivable are lost due to ignorance of purpose.

7. Our lifestyle should be determined by the recognition of the gifts, proper development and utilization of these gifts so maximum benefits accrue to mankind and the Creator is pleased. We are to manage our lives according to the expectations of the Giver of His many sided gifts (wisdom, grace, talents, etc.). Proverbs 10:4-5.

Proverbs 10:4-5

He who has a slack hand becomes poor, But the hand of the diligent makes rich.

He who gathers in summer is a wise son;

He who sleeps in harvest is a son who causes shame.

Faithfulness, excellence and productive efforts at stewardship should characterise our lifestyle.

God is the source of all good things and there are channels around us through which these things come to us. God uses channels to get through to us but many confuse their channels and consider them as source.

Stewardship and Multiplication. (How to increase in anything and how to sustain the increase.)

God is interested in our coming into increase. Remember the Lord thy God for it is He who causes you to prosper. I wish above all that you prosper and be in health even as your soul prospers. The love of money is the root of all evil. I have learnt to abase and abound, I can do all things through Christ who strengthens me. My God shall supply all your needs according to His riches in glory by Christ Jesus. (Deut. 8:18, 3John 2, 1Tim. 6: 10-17, Phil. 4:10-19.)

Principles of Increase in any area of life!

1. Increase or success or prosperity starts from inside not from outside.

3 John 2

Beloved, I pray that you may prosper in all things and be in health, just as your soul prospers.

Poverty is also an inside issue. The phrase, as your soul prospers, implies that the issues of life are from within not without. Proverbs 4, tells us to guard our hearts with all diligence for out of it flows issues of life. So many spend their time taking care of the external parts of their lives and pay little attention to the internal parts. Failure is as a result of making many wrong choices over time. Success is as a result of making right choices and being disciplined to stay with them. Our choices are a product of the operating mentality of our lives. Our thoughts, perceptions, opinions and desires are all inside us. Our self image also matters. Our nature, nurture and environment (culture) have all contributed to how we see ourselves and how we see things around us.

We all see things according to what we are on the inside. Many are failures going somewhere to happen. When we allow God's word to form our operating mentality, God's wisdom through the application of His Word will put us over in life.

2. The second principle of increase is called the "law of sowing and reaping". Everything obeys this law. We sow thoughts to reap words, we sow words to reap actions, we sow actions to reap habits and our habits are like horses that take us into our future. The inputs we allow into our lives through reading and association will ultimately affect our choices in life. Repeated actions are known to form ingrained habits. It all starts with thoughts.

When a person receives Christ and gets exposed to foundational truth as per what Christ has done for us and who we now become as well as the quality of our relationship with God our Father, such input will begin to condition such a person and they won't see themselves as they were before but as new creatures in Christ. (see our teachings on who we are in Christ and the Cross the place of exchange on my website www.kolaewuosho.com, and the Ministry's website : www.fowm.org).

Give what you need! Give yourself to God through service in His kingdom. You will become more of what He wants you to become as you give yourself so He can use you to reach other lives.

3. The 3rd principle is "knowing God as your source". I have learnt to abase and abound, not moved by my physical circumstances but staying connected to my source, I can handle any situation that comes. Since God is my source, my channels can change, dry up or be productive, I am still the same, no matter what. This freedom to be myself and still do what is right is a major key to my stewardship and my staying prosperous. With a solid connection to your source you can still do what is supposed to be done no matter what. There are many lessons to learn in this phase. This is when you refuse to stop giving, or sowing even when it looks like it's not producing.

Your job is a channel not your source. God is your source and He can change channels.

4. Preserving your harvest. When it is a matter of money we need to learn how to spend less than we generate or earn. We also need to be open to other channels of income. He gives seed to the sower and bread to the eater, knowing what is meant for eating and what is meant for sowing will go a long way to help in helping us to preserve our harvests. Our obedience to God in how we spend money to honor Him is crucial if we are to maintain the flow.

    4a. Tithing is the first discipline in managing money, it progresses to sowing and reaping of financial seeds regularly. There are different types of giving in scriptures: giving to the poor; giving for the furtherance of the gospel; tithing and partnering with ministries. Phil. 4:16-19.

4b. Maintaining the flow calls for cultivating the lifestyle, based on accurate knowledge of how the issue operates. Poverty manifests itself in certain ways of thinking: a not-enough attitude; self pity; laziness with a victim's attitude; wasteful spending and thoughtless or reckless lifestyle. Prosperity will manifest in exactly opposite these qualities. It has an abundance mentality, not greedy or selfish. It is characterized by diligence and integrity.

5. The soldier, farmer and athlete.

2 Timothy 2:1-7 (AMP)

1 SO YOU, my son, be strong (strengthened inwardly) in the grace (spiritual blessing) that is [to be found only] in Christ Jesus.

2 And the [instructions] which you have heard from me along with many witnesses, transmit and entrust [as a deposit] to reliable and faithful men who will be competent and qualified to teach others also. 3 Take [with me] your share of the hardships and suffering [which you are called to endure] as a good (first-class) soldier of Christ Jesus.

4 No soldier when in service gets entangled in the enterprises of [civilian] life; his aim is to satisfy and please the one who enlisted him.

5 And if anyone enters competitive games, he is not crowned unless he competes lawfully (fairly, according to the rules laid down). 6 [It is] the hard-working farmer [who labors to produce] who must be the first partaker of the fruits.

7 Think over these things I am saying [understand them and grasp their application], for the Lord will grant you full insight and understanding in everything.

2 Timothy 2:1-7 (NKJV)

Be Strong in Grace

1 You therefore, my son, be strong in the grace that is in Christ Jesus.
2 And the things that you have heard from me among many witnesses,

commit these to faithful men who will be able to teach others also. 3 You therefore must endure hardship as a good soldier of Jesus Christ. 4 No one engaged in warfare entangles himself with the affairs of this life, that he may please him who enlisted him as a soldier. 5 And also if anyone competes in athletics, he is not crowned unless he competes according to the rules. 6 The hardworking farmer must be first to partake of the crops. 7 Consider what I say, and may the Lord give you understanding in all things.

The three activities that characterize victorious Christianity as captured by apostle Paul in his letter to Timothy are the Farmer, the Soldier and the Athlete. The farmer sows the right seeds in correct quantities in the right soil treated to produce. The soldier, at the beck and call of the government is always battle ready. The athlete remains ever ready as they prepare for competitions. In our lives we need to know how to sow the right seeds in the right soils and the correct quantities. We need to know how to resist the thoughts of poverty and all negative patterns in our lives. We need to stay spiritually fit for whatever challenges await us in life.

Enduring hardness is involved in being battle ready in committing to principles that will bring about godly progress in our lives. Not yielding to the flesh, the worldly spirits and the demonic realms all call for hardness on ourselves.

Training, studying and practise doing God's word is as intense as an athlete preparing for a competition. Renewing the mind is more than reading the bible, it takes being a doer of the word to actually reconfigure the mind. Sowing the right seeds as discussed is likened to a farmer sowing with the mind of reaping a harvest. The best seed to sow is God's word. Sow it into your heart and expect to harvest Christlikeness!

Romans 12:1-2

Living Sacrifices to God

I beseech you therefore, brethren, by the mercies of God, that you present your bodies a living sacrifice, holy, acceptable to God, which is your reasonable service. And do not be conformed to this world, but be transformed by the renewing of your mind, that you may prove what is that good and acceptable and perfect will of God.

James 1:21-25 (NKJV)

Doers-Not Hearers Only

21 Therefore lay aside all filthiness and overflow of wickedness, and receive with meekness the implanted word, which is able to save your souls.

22 But be doers of the word, and not hearers only, deceiving yourselves. 23 For if anyone is a hearer of the word and not a doer, he is like a man observing his natural face in a mirror; 24 for he observes himself, goes away, and immediately forgets what kind of man he was. 25 But he who looks into the perfect law of liberty and continues in it, and is not a forgetful hearer but a doer of the work, this one will be blessed in what he does.

Learn to be a steward of your life, relationships, time, talent and treasures. Learn how God wants you to operate in life. God is love and love gives, as we seek the highest good for others. We develop our potential through personal and spiritual development. As we develop, we grow in understanding and become a better and greater influence in the lives of others through our leadership development. Set goals for activities that will grow you up as you steward everything in your life. Even opportunities need stewarding too. God bless you as you learn to steward all He has invested in you.

Luke 2:52

And Jesus increased in wisdom and stature, and in favor with God and men.

REFLECTING ON STEWARDSHIP Lessons from chapter 4.

In maximising our leadership potential, understanding and walking in the principles of Stewardship becomes vital to our productivity in life. Stewardship has the keys to effective leadership, the keys to increase in every good thing in our lives, and knowing that we can count on God's grace to enable us steward everything He has made available to us through His plans and purposes. We are stewards utilising God's generosity towards us to bring Him glory and honour as He sees us fulfil His purposes in our lives and in the lives of people around us.

CHAPTER 5

Embracing Kingdom Vision

THERE IS A place for personal vision in the kingdom of God. When we understand the place of personal vision, it becomes very practical that we can comprehend the vision of God's kingdom for our lives.

The starting point is in understanding God's kingdom and operations of the kingdom on planet earth. There is a past expression, present day expression and then a future expression of the kingdom of God. How do we see the various expressions of God's kingdom on earth? God has always worked through people who are yielded to Him, despite their human limitations.

The Kingdom Vision is God's plan for your life. Identifying your purpose for being on earth, happens when you give your self completely to serving God and adding value to people through your relationship with God. Your contributions have something to do with the overall picture of God's kingdom. When David killed Goliath, he went beyond achieving a personal vision, then went on to accomplish a bigger vision for the nation, that was a type of embracing a kingdom vision. The larger body benefits from your service and contributions. That is a type of kingdom vision. Once you embrace a kingdom vision, no sacrifice will be too great to make.

Goliath made His boasts.

1 Samuel 17:10-11 (NKJV)

10 And the Philistine said, "I defy the armies of Israel this day; give me a man, that we may fight together." When Saul and all Israel heard these words of the Philistine, they were dismayed and greatly afraid.

One of the greatest hindrances to embracing kingdom vision, is the opportunity for offences. Offences can hinder the flow of God's power, Anointing and purposes in people's lives. David had to deal with the opportunity of not being offended by his own brother.

1 Samuel 17:25-30 (NKJV)

25 So the men of Israel said, "Have you seen this man who has come up? Surely he has come up to defy Israel; and it shall be that the man who kills him the king will enrich with great riches, will give him his daughter, and give his father's house exemption from taxes in Israel."

26 Then David spoke to the men who stood by him, saying, "What shall be done for the man who kills this Philistine and takes away the reproach from Israel? For who is this uncircumcised Philistine, that he should defy the armies of the living God?"

27 And the people answered him in this manner, saying, "So shall it be done for the man who kills him."

28 Now Eliab his oldest brother heard when he spoke to the men; and Eliab's anger was aroused against David, and he said, "Why did you come down here? And with whom have you left those few sheep in the wilderness? I know your pride and the insolence of your heart, for you have come down to see the battle."

29 And David said, "What have I done now? Is there not a cause?" 30 Then he turned from him toward another and said the same thing; and these people answered him as the first ones did.

David had a revelation of his covenant relationship and privileges with God, and his testimonies of God's deliverance in other matters helped his confidence. These are all lessons we need to step into the bigger picture of kingdom vision. Dealing with offence is major, having an understanding of our covenant relationship with God through Christ Jesus, then being willing to be used of God to bring deliverance and joy to His people and glory to His name.

1 Samuel 17:31-37 (NKJV)

31 Now when the words which David spoke were heard, they reported them to Saul; and he sent for him. 32 Then David said to Saul, "Let no man's heart fail because of him; your servant will go and fight with this Philistine."

33 And Saul said to David, "You are not able to go against this Philistine to fight with him; for you are a youth, and he a man of war from his youth."

34 But David said to Saul, "Your servant used to keep his father's sheep, and when a lion or a bear came and took a lamb out of the flock, 35 I went out after it and struck it, and delivered the lamb from its mouth; and when it arose against me, I caught it by its beard, and struck and killed it. 36 Your servant has killed both lion and bear; and this uncircumcised Philistine will be like one of them, seeing he has defied the armies of the living God." 37 Moreover David said, "The Lord, who delivered me from the paw of the lion and from the paw of the bear, He will deliver me from the hand of this Philistine."

And Saul said to David, "Go, and the Lord be with you!"

Another lesson here is that we should not try using an amour that we have not used before. David did not use Saul's armour. We are to use what we have been using that has been tried and tested. In the development process we learn to engage everything we have from our faculties to our elements of grace, like the name of Jesus as well as other weapons of our warfare. Use them in smaller matters so you have confidence in bigger matters.

1 Samuel 17:38-40 (NKJV)

38 So Saul clothed David with his armour, and he put a bronze helmet on his head; he also clothed him with a coat of mail. 39 David fastened his sword to his armour and tried to walk, for he had not tested them. And David said to Saul, "I cannot walk with these, for I have not tested them." So David took them off.

40 Then he took his staff in his hand; and he chose for himself five smooth stones from the brook, and put them in a shepherd's bag, in a pouch which he had, and his sling was in his hand. And he drew near to the Philistine.

There is no doubt in my mind that David was under the influence of the Holy Spirit. No normal human being would imagine a stone killing a giant. Even when his stone was a point of mockery in the face of the giant, the young boy was still convinced that it's not the stone but the name of the Lord that will do the job.

1 Samuel 17:42-47 (NKJV)

42 And when the Philistine looked about and saw David, he disdained him; for he was only a youth, ruddy and good-looking. 43 So the Philistine said to David, "Am I a dog, that you come to me with sticks?" 44 And the Philistine cursed David by his gods. And the Philistine said to David, "Come to me, and I will give your flesh to the birds of the air and the beasts of the field!"

45 Then David said to the Philistine, "You come to me with a sword, with a spear, and with a javelin. But I come to you in the name of the Lord of hosts, the God of the armies of Israel, whom you have defied. 46 This day the Lord will deliver you into my hand, and I will strike you and take your head from you. And this day I will give the carcasses of the camp of the Philistines to the birds of the air and the wild beasts of the earth, that all the earth may know that there is a God in Israel. 47 Then all this assembly shall know that the Lord does not save with sword and spear; for the battle is the Lord's, and He will give you into our hands."

WAR OF WORDS.

David's faith was doing the speaking and his conviction, confidence and full persuasion was that the giant was as good as dead as far as he was concerned. He pronounced his death before he took any action. Remember that the giant was also doing his own speaking. In enlarging your coast in your service to God, get ready for a war of words. He cursed David by his gods and pronounced death on David. David did the same over him. Never let the enemy have the last say, always reply him. David had confidence in his God's ability to deliver him from this giant and to bring an end to this defiance to the God of Israel. He knew His God stands up for His name to be honoured in the land and lives of His people. Kingdom vision honours the King of the kingdom.

1 Samuel 17:48-51 (NKJV)

48 So it was, when the Philistine arose and came and drew near to meet David, that David hurried and ran toward the army to meet the Philistine. 49 Then David put his hand in his bag and took out a stone; and he slung it and struck the Philistine in his forehead, so that the stone sank into his forehead, and he fell on his face to the earth. 50 So David prevailed over the Philistine with a sling and a stone, and struck the Philistine and killed him. But there was no sword in the hand of David. 51 Therefore David ran and stood over the Philistine, took his sword and drew it out of its sheath and killed him, and cut off his head with it.

And when the Philistines saw that their champion was dead, they fled.

There is always a battle for any kingdom vision to be fulfilled. There are lessons to learn. There is a growing up to be rightly positioned. So we must be battle ready, full of wisdom and stay confident in God to handle our challenges as we embrace kingdom vision.

Satan uses many things to stop the flow of God's power into any situation. He starts by using persecution and affliction to stop the productivity of the word in the hearts of believers. Then he uses offences to stop the flow of power like he did in the days when our Lord Jesus was on earth.

Jesu was definitely anointed by God but could not do much when unbelief and offence were present.

Acts 10:38

how God anointed Jesus of Nazareth with the Holy Spirit and with power, who went about doing good and healing all who were oppressed by the devil, for God was with Him.

Matthew 13:53-58 (NKJV)

Jesus Rejected at Nazareth

(Mark 6:1–6; Luke 4:16–30)

53 Now it came to pass, when Jesus had finished these parables, that He departed from there. 54 When He had come to His own country, He taught them in their synagogue, so that they were astonished and

said, "Where did this Man get this wisdom and these mighty works? 55 Is this not the carpenter's son? Is not His mother called Mary? And His brothers James, Joses, Simon, and Judas? 56 And His sisters, are they not all with us? Where then did this Man get all these things?" 57 So they were offended at Him.

But Jesus said to them, "A prophet is not without honor except in his own country and in his own house." 58 Now He did not do many mighty works there because of their unbelief.

"There" is the place of unbelief and offence. He could do no mighty miracles there even though he was anointed. Offence stopped the flow of the Anointing.

In being battle ready we need to know how to prevent the word from being unproductive in our lives.

Mark 4:14-20 (AMP)

14 The sower sows the Word.

15 The ones along the path are those who have the Word sown [in their hearts], but when they hear, Satan comes at once and [by force] takes away the message which is sown in them.

16 And in the same way the ones sown upon stony ground are those who, when they hear the Word, at once receive and accept and welcome it with joy;

17 And they have no real root in themselves, and so they endure for a little while; then when trouble or persecution arises on account of the Word, they immediately are offended (become displeased, indignant, resentful) and they stumble and fall away.

18 And the ones sown among the thorns are others who hear the Word;

19 Then the cares and anxieties of the world and distractions of the age, and the pleasure and delight and false glamour and deceitfulness of riches, and the craving and passionate desire for other things creep in and choke and suffocate the Word, and it becomes fruitless.

20 And those sown on the good (well-adapted) soil are the ones who hear the Word and receive and accept and welcome it and bear fruit—some thirty times as much as was sown, some sixty times as much, and some [even] a hundred times as much.

Three times out of four the word was rendered unproductive. The enemy uses cares and anxieties to steal the word (containing the wisdom, power, and purposes) of God from the hearts of listeners.

So both the presence and power (Anointing) and the word of purpose can be aborted in the lives of people, through offences and other things we see in these scriptures.

This book is designed to equip you to handle all these things and be victorious in life.

REFLECTING ON THE LESSONS learnt in chapter 5 on Kingdom vision.

Kingdom vision is your getting to know you have a role to play in God's program. Kingdom vision is about measuring value to God, His kingdom, His people and in fulfilling His purposes. You must have the right identity of yourself. You are an agent of the Kingdom. The power of the kingdom is at your disposal. Your faith and disposition of obedience and honour to God remain as skills we need to develop in our lives if we shall fulfil God's kingdom vision. Do not allow offences or any other work of the flesh to hinder the flow of God's power in and through your life, in prayers and labour of love to meet the needs of others.

Your faith and disposition of obedience and honour remain as skills you need to develop in your life if you shall fulfill God's kingdom vision.

CHAPTER 6

Teamwork

I T NEVER CEASES to amaze me in how much team work we see in the church at Jerusalem and most of the book of Acts. Team work seems to be the stabilising factor, as well as the diversity in the united front that advances the kingdom of God. The identity or peculiarity of the individual is not lost, if anything, it is enhanced. I am thrilled to read that God can speak to one and all members of his team consider it a call for all from God.

Acts 16:9-10 (NKJV)

9 And a vision appeared to Paul in the night. A man of Macedonia stood and pleaded with him, saying, "Come over to Macedonia and help us." 10 Now after he had seen the vision, immediately we sought to go to Macedonia, concluding that the Lord had called us to preach the gospel to them.

To appreciate team work you can start by studying to see that Jesus sent them out in twos during His earthly ministry. What about the early church always allowing decisions to be influenced by the team before final decisions are arrived. They had their own company.

Acts 4:23-32 (NKJV)

Prayer for Boldness (cf. Ps. 2:1, 2)

23 And being let go, they went to their own companions and reported all that the chief priests and elders had said to them. 24 So when they

heard that, they raised their voice to God with one accord and said: "Lord, You are God, who made heaven and earth and the sea, and all that is in them, 25 who by the mouth of Your servant David have said:

'Why did the nations rage,
And the people plot vain things?

26 The kings of the earth took their stand, And the rulers were gathered together Against the Lord and against His Christ.'

27 "For truly against Your holy Servant Jesus, whom You anointed, both Herod and Pontius Pilate, with the Gentiles and the people of Israel, were gathered together 28 to do whatever Your hand and Your purpose determined before to be done. 29 Now, Lord, look on their threats, and grant to Your servants that with all boldness they may speak Your word, 30 by stretching out Your hand to heal, and that signs and wonders may be done through the name of Your holy Servant Jesus."

31 And when they had prayed, the place where they were assembled together was shaken; and they were all filled with the Holy Spirit, and they spoke the word of God with boldness.
    Sharing in All Things

32 Now the multitude of those who believed were of one heart and one soul; neither did anyone say that any of the things he possessed was his own, but they had all things in common.

They were united in heart and spirit and had all things in common. From the early chapters of the book of Acts we see team work, unity as well as individual gifting not intimidating others or producing pride in the one demonstrating the power.
    See Peter healing the man by the gate beautiful.

Acts 3:4-13 (NKJV)

4 And fixing his eyes on him, with John, Peter said, "Look at us." 5 So he gave them his attention, expecting to receive something from them. 6 Then Peter said, "Silver and gold I do not have, but what I do have I give you: In the name of Jesus Christ of Nazareth, rise up and walk." 7 And he took him by the right hand and lifted him up, and immediately his feet and ankle

bones received strength. 8 So he, leaping up, stood and walked and entered the temple with them—walking, leaping, and praising God. 9 And all the people saw him walking and praising God. 10 Then they knew that it was he who sat begging alms at the Beautiful Gate of the temple; and they were filled with wonder and amazement at what had happened to him.

Preaching in Solomon's Portico

11 Now as the lame man who was healed held on to Peter and John, all the people ran together to them in the porch which is called Solomon's, greatly amazed. 12 So when Peter saw it, he responded to the people: "Men of Israel, why do you marvel at this? Or why look so intently at us, as though by our own power or godliness we had made this man walk? 13 The God of Abraham, Isaac, and Jacob, the God of our fathers, glorified His Servant Jesus, whom you delivered up and denied in the presence of Pilate, when he was determined to let Him go.

What made it possible for them to have one accord and respected each person's gifts without envy or jealousy and the individual not feeling proud and above others? I believe it is the doing of the Holy Spirit on their hearts and their allowing Him do His bidding in them. Also there was mutual respect as well as mutual acceptance of each other. No competition, no strife, no showmanship of any sort. All God, not man to take any glory. You notice that the spirit of unity usually preceded the manifestation of God's grace and power in their situations.

Great Grace comes in the midst of unity.

Acts 4:32-35 (NKJV)

Sharing in All Things

32 Now the multitude of those who believed were of one heart and one soul; neither did anyone say that any of the things he possessed was his own, but they had all things in common. 33 And with great power the apostles gave witness to the resurrection of the Lord Jesus. And great grace was upon them all. 34 Nor was there anyone among them who lacked; for all who were possessors of lands or houses sold them, and brought the proceeds of the things that were sold, 35 and laid them at the apostles' feet; and they distributed to each as anyone had need.

Can we be inspired by the gifting in others without envying them? Advantages of team work.

Each person can focus on the area of their strength so the team can get great results as each give their best effort in carrying out their assignments.

Each will not be burdened in areas where they have no ability as the team divides responsibility as each has strength.

Together the team can accomplish more than if one person was saddled with the responsibility.

Different perspectives from others can impact and improve our perspectives on any matter.

The support and encouragement we receive from one another in the team are immeasurable.

Matters can be discussed and different perspectives are considered so the eventual outcome will be richly accomplished due to many people's input.

Appreciating team work in effective leadership.

Acts 13:2-7 (NKJV)

2 As they ministered to the Lord and fasted, the Holy Spirit said, "Now separate to Me Barnabas and Saul for the work to which I have called them." 3 Then, having fasted and prayed, and laid hands on them, they sent them away.

Preaching in Cyprus

4 So, being sent out by the Holy Spirit, they went down to Seleucia, and from there they sailed to Cyprus. 5 And when they arrived in Salamis, they preached the word of God in the synagogues of the Jews. They also had John as their assistant.

6 Now when they had gone through the island to Paphos, they found a certain sorcerer, a false prophet, a Jew whose name was Bar-Jesus, 7 who was with the proconsul, Sergius Paulus, an intelligent man. This man called for Barnabas and Saul and sought to hear the word of God.

We see from their calling, they were called as a team of ministers. In the book of Acts we read many leadership positions being shared amongst people like Elders, or shepherds. There is usually a sense of plurality in the leadership of the early church.

REFLECTING on the lessons learnt in chapter 6 on Teamwork.

Team work makes the dream work. The multifaceted nature of life, ministry and leadership calls for a recognition of roles as individuals are encouraged to belong to a team and their effectiveness is not minimised as each will be supported by others as they also experience support from others to fulfil their roles. The team is better off in the overall sense.

CHAPTER 7

Recognising Godly Boundaries

STEWARDSHIP, TEAMWORK AND these fine qualities demands from us a recognition of boundaries that will make for successful leadership operations in our relationships with others.

Every thing we do and have are designed to function right within certain boundaries. All our faculties were designed to function within boundaries if they will remain healthy. Recognition of such boundaries and working within them is a major part of our understanding and maturing process. Think of healthy boundaries for the thoughts we allow in our minds. Now there are avenues for enlarging healthy boundaries in certain fields but learning about them and how they operate is vital to our sustainable growth.

In relationships, healthy boundaries make for Godly relationships. Joseph is a case study in this regard.

Genesis 39:2-9 (NKJV)

2 The Lord was with Joseph, and he was a successful man; and he was in the house of his master the Egyptian. 3 And his master saw that the Lord was with him and that the Lord made all he did to prosper in his hand. 4 So Joseph found favor in his sight, and served him. Then he made him overseer of his house, and all that he had he put under his authority. 5 So it was, from the time that he had made him overseer of his house and all that he had, that the Lord blessed the Egyptian's house for Joseph's sake; and the blessing of the Lord was on all that he had in the house and in the field. 6 Thus he left all that he had in

Joseph's hand, and he did not know what he had except for the bread which he ate.

Now Joseph was handsome in form and appearance.

7 And it came to pass after these things that his master's wife cast longing eyes on Joseph, and she said, "Lie with me."

8 But he refused and said to his master's wife, "Look, my master does not know what is with me in the house, and he has committed all that he has to my hand. 9 There is no one greater in this house than I, nor has he kept back anything from me but you, because you are his wife. How then can I do this great wickedness, and sin against God?"

Without a maturing process, Joseph could have allowed his success get into his head and become proud and so forget the healthy boundaries drawn by his convictions and in honour of his boss. He refused to sleep with the wife of his boss and was conscious of not sinning against God.

The principle of boundaries should affect everything we do. Knowing our limitations simply helps us see the need for others in our lives. Allowing Godly boundaries help us stay true to God and to ourselves as well as our purposes in God.

Boundaries represent well placed limitations that are adequate to enhance our productivity and effectiveness in life. For instance we can only be disciplined in our thoughts when we regulate what we pay attention to in our minds. If we allow every thought that flies around to stay in our minds, we may be setting ourselves up for failure in life. So we create certain conditions that are determined by the kind of thoughts we allow. When we define those thoughts that we want to allow, whatever parameter we use to define and so allow ourselves to think, these parameters define the boundaries we place on our minds. The same is true for our words, even our relationships with others.

REFLECTING ON LESSONS learnt from chapter 7: <u>understanding Godly boundaries.</u>

Have you set boundaries over your thoughts, words and actions..? What informed your boundaries? Are you able to be consistent in the operation of set boundaries?

CHAPTER 8

Dealing with pride, insecurity and allowing others to make their contributions.

IN DEVELOPING OUR leadership potential, one enemy we must contend with is something our human flesh enjoys. It is called Pride.

It is the secret operator of many other sins in our lives.

Doorway of pride and how to deal with pride.

Pride is the deadliest enemy of the christian today! There is not a single Christian alive who doesn't have to deal with the spirit of pride on a regular basis. Our flesh wants to be exalted, recognised and admired. It wants to be looked up to by other people. That's just one of the truth about the clay vessels our spirits inhabit.

Pride has been called the father of all sin, and it is not hard to see why. Lucifer experienced pride. Isaiah 14:13 "I will exalt my throne above the stars of God."

Pride says "I am right and I want to have things my own way". Pride is the tendency to exalt self; it is the most poisonous evil a Christian must deal with.

"There is no greater pride than seeking to humiliate ourselves beyond measure! And sometimes there is no greater humility than to attempt great works for God." Humility is exalting God through the accomplishments He produces in your life. Without God you cannot be or do anything but in Christ there is absolutely nothing you cannot do.

1 Corinthians 1:29 says no flesh should glory in His presence.

Pride is the biggest challenge and the hardest thing to identify in our lives. It takes courage.

King Saul's example

2 Samuel 1:19-21 (AMP)

19 Your glory, O Israel, is slain upon your high places. How have the mighty fallen!

20 Tell it not in Gath, announce it not in the streets of Ashkelon, lest the daughters of the Philistines rejoice, lest the daughters of the uncircumcised exult.

21 O mountains of Gilboa, let there be no dew or rain upon you, or fields with offerings. For there the shield of the mighty was defiled, the shield of Saul, as though he were not anointed with oil.

Here he was completely defeated. Satan cannot defeat us if he does not deceive us first. Saul opened the door of pride. Humility is the main quality that makes us useful in God's kingdom.

Lies and exaggerations. 1 Samuel 13:3-4 (AMP)

Jonathan smote the Philistine garrison at Geba, and the Philistines heard of it. And Saul blew the trumpet throughout all the land, saying, Let the Hebrews hear!

4 All Israel heard that Saul had defeated the Philistine garrison and also that Israel had become an abomination to the Philistines. And the people were called out to join Saul at Gilgal.

Jonathan smote the garrison of the philistines and Saul took the credit! He was insecure with his own identity and position with God, so he lied to make himself look better in the eyes of the people. We need to deal with this insecurity in our lives, it may want us to exaggerate or even lie about ourselves in order to elevate ourselves in the eyes of others.

Impatience and arrogance. 1 Samuel 13:8-9 (AMP)

Saul waited seven days, according to the set time Samuel had appointed. But Samuel had not come to Gilgal, and the people were scattering from Saul.

9 So Saul said, Bring me the burnt offering and the peace offerings. And he offered the burnt offering [which he was forbidden to do].

Saul arrogantly tried to assume the office and anointing of another man, the prophet. Impatience comes up when we fail to wait for God's timing for our lives. Don't help God by trying to emulate someone you really respect rather than becoming who God wants you to be. Stay within your anointing and calling. Wait on God to promote you. Consecrate yourself not only to God's plan but also His timing.

1 Samuel 15:3-9 (AMP)

3 Now go and smite Amalek and utterly destroy all they have; do not spare them, but kill both man and woman, infant and suckling, ox and sheep, camel and donkey.

4 So Saul assembled the men and numbered them at Telaim— 200,000 men on foot and 10,000 men of Judah.

5 And Saul came to the city of Amalek and laid wait in the valley. 6 Saul warned the Kenites, Go, depart, get down from among the Amalekites, lest I destroy you with them; for you showed kindness to all the Israelites when they came up out of Egypt. So the Kenites departed from among the Amalekites.

7 Saul smote the Amalekites from Havilah as far as Shur, which is east of Egypt.

8 And he took Agag king of the Amalekites alive, though he utterly destroyed all the rest of the people with the sword.

9 Saul and the people spared Agag and the best of the sheep, oxen, fatlings, lambs, and all that was good, and would not utterly destroy them; but all that was undesirable or worthless they destroyed utterly.

A low regard for God's word. 1 Sam. 15:3-9 (AMP). Saul felt free to disregard the command of The Lord for the sake of gaining popularity with the people. This is a lack of reverence for God's command.

1 Samuel 15:20-23(AMP)

20 Saul said to Samuel, Yes, I have obeyed the voice of the Lord and have gone the way which the Lord sent me, and have brought Agag king of Amalek and have utterly destroyed the Amalekites.

21 But the people took from the spoil sheep and oxen, the chief of the things to be utterly destroyed, to sacrifice to the Lord your God in Gilgal.

22 Samuel said, Has the Lord as great a delight in burnt offerings and sacrifices as in obeying the voice of the Lord? Behold, to obey is better than sacrifice, and to hearken than the fat of rams.

23 For rebellion is as the sin of witchcraft, and stubbornness is as idolatry and teraphim (household good luck images). Because you have rejected the word of the Lord, He also has rejected you from being king.
Blame shifting verses 20/21.
Saul shifted the blame on the people like Adam did in the garden.

Genesis 3:12 (AMP).

We need to take responsibility for our actions. Sacrifice instead of obedience. Verses 21-22.
To obey is better than sacrifice. Our sacrifice is Christ on the cross so we can confess our sins but its still better to obey than continue to confess the same sins day and night. Decide to obey . Any other life style is a revelation of pride at work in us.
We are more susceptible to pride in the areas of our natural strengths than in how we deal with people in relationships.

HOW to Deal with Pride.

Develop an attitude of contentment. This is the antidote to the spirit of dissatisfaction. Adam was dissatisfied with his lot in the garden, he wanted to be like God. He disobeyed God because of pride.

"Be satisfied with your present circumstances" Hebrews 13:5 (AMP). See 1 Timothy 6:6-8 (AMP).

[And it is, indeed, a source of immense profit, for] godliness accompanied with contentment (that contentment which is a sense of inward sufficiency) is great and abundant gain.

7 For we brought nothing into the world, and obviously we cannot take anything out of the world;

8 But if we have food and clothing, with these we shall be content (satisfied).

See Philippians 4:11 (AMP) I learn to be content.

Philippians 4:11-13 (AMP)

Not that I am implying that I was in any personal want, for I have learned how to be content (satisfied to the point where I am not disturbed or disquieted) in whatever state I am.

12 I know how to be abased and live humbly in straitened circumstances, and I know also how to enjoy plenty and live in abundance. I have learned in any and all circumstances the secret of facing every situation, whether well- fed or going hungry, having a sufficiency and enough to spare or going without and being in want.

13 I have strength for all things in Christ Who empowers me [I am ready for anything and equal to anything through Him Who infuses inner strength into me; I am self- sufficient in Christ's sufficiency].

In Philippians 3:14 (AMP) he presses toward the mark. See 4:6-7 too. Fight the good fight of faith and lay hold on eternal life. See 1 Timothy 6:12 (AMP).

Fight the good fight of the faith; lay hold of the eternal life to which you were summoned and [for which] you confessed the good confession [of faith] before many witnesses. Philippians 3:14 (AMP)

I press on toward the goal to win the [supreme and heavenly] prize to which God in Christ Jesus is calling us upward.

The mark is servant hood.

Luke 22:26

But this is not to be so with you; on the contrary, let him who is the greatest among you become like the youngest, and him who is the chief and leader like one who serves.

Service is the key to maintaining the outward focus. Jesus demonstrated this by washing their feet in John 13:3-15 (AMP). The mark is what will keep you on course.

If we are going to win the prize of zoe life, we need to think differently about servanthood. When you begin serving with your money, giving, you will begin winning in the area of finances. When you begin serving in the area of relationships, loving, you will begin to win a harvest of love in your life. The more you press into the mark of service the more you move into God's marvellous zoe life.

Servant hood releases the power of God into our lives as seen in Isaiah 40:29-31 (AMP).

Isaiah 40:29-30 (AMP)

He gives power to the faint and weary, and to him who has no might He increases strength [causing it to multiply and making it to abound].

30 Even youths shall faint and be weary, and [selected] young men shall feebly stumble and fall exhausted;

Isaiah 40:31 (AMP)

But those who wait for the Lord [who expect, look for, and hope in Him] shall change and renew their strength and power; they shall lift their wings and mount up [close to God] as eagles [mount up to the sun]; they shall run and not be weary, they shall walk and not faint or become tired.

To wait on The Lord is likened to a servant waiting on the one he serves. As we serve God, His power is released into our lives and situation.

As we wait upon God's needs and purposes on the earth, as we serve Him, expecting Him to empower us, He will release the might we need to be winners in every circumstance.

Job's life proved that. In Chapter 42, after all he had suffered, he turned outward to pray for his friends. He began to serve the needs of others rather than focusing on his own needs, the power of God was released immediately into his circumstances. He was healed and prospered double. The power of God will open doors for anyone who presses into the mark of servanthood.

Paul also talks about forgetting the things behind. verse 13. If you are mindful of past mistakes and failures we will not press on to the mark of the high calling in Christ Jesus. It is important to deal with dissatisfaction as it is usually rooted in the past. Forget the past and press unto the mark of the prize of the high calling by becoming a servant at heart.

GOD WILL NOT LEAVE YOU HELPLESS

The second point of view you need to overcome the temptation to be disturbed and disquieted.

Hebrews 13:5 (AMP)

Let your character or moral disposition be free from love of money [including greed, avarice, lust, and craving for earthly possessions] and be satisfied with your present [circumstances and with what you have]; for He [God] Himself has said, I will not in any way fail you nor give you up nor leave you without support. [I will] not, [I will] not, [I will] not in any degree leave you helpless nor forsake nor let [you] down (relax My hold on you)! [Assuredly not!]

You need time to grow.

Luke 2:52 (AMP)

And Jesus increased in wisdom (in broad and full understanding) and in stature and years, and in favor with God and man.

Your ability to handle what God wants to give you, will determine when you get it so be patient. Growth takes time. Let God continue to prepare you for the next level by pressing toward the mark that He sets before you. Remain content, close the door to pride by eliminating dissatisfaction.

DEVELOP A HEART OF GRATITUDE.

Romans 1:21-22 (AMP)

Because when they knew and recognized Him as God, they did not honor and glorify Him as God or give Him thanks. But instead they became futile and godless in their thinking [with vain imaginings, foolish reasoning, and stupid speculations] and their senseless minds were darkened.

22 Claiming to be wise, they became fools [professing to be smart, they made simpletons of themselves].

You will be prideful if you are not thankful. Make a quality decision to be thankful for what God has already given not being focussed on what you don't have. If you constantly think on the negative you will not be thankful and will end up being bitter and resentful. The root of all this is pride-and that pride is based on the assumption that you deserve better. Is God not just? Start looking daily for a blessing for which you can be thankful. Resist the temptation to call other people's attention to your situation in order to get a little pity from them.

Build upon your foundation of contentment a house of thanksgiving to God for all His blessings in your life. Become someone who has a heart of gratitude, and you will close a major door to pride and deception in your life.

TRUE HUMILITY

True bible humility is a recognition that without God you are nothing but that with God, you can do absolutely anything-and give Him all the glory for it. Biblical humility eliminates the 'me,myself and i' orientation in your life. It removes selfishness as a motivation for the things you do. Selfishness is almost a synonym for pride. This is called dying to self. It is a putting to death of the tendency of your flesh to motivate you to serve your own interests.

1 Peter 5:5-6

Likewise, you who are younger and of lesser rank, be subject to the elders (the ministers and spiritual guides of the church) — [giving them due respect and yielding to their counsel]. Clothe (apron) yourselves, all of you, with humility [as the garb of a servant, so that its covering cannot possibly be stripped from you, with freedom from pride and arrogance] toward one another. For God sets Himself against the proud (the insolent, the overbearing, the disdainful, the presumptuous, the boastful) — [and He opposes, frustrates, and defeats them], but gives grace (favor, blessing) to the humble.

6 Therefore humble yourselves [demote, lower yourselves in your own estimation] under the mighty hand of God, that in due time He may exalt you.

Pride opens the door to satan and causes God to resist you! Humility is the key to walking in God's increase and sustain His blessings. If you humble yourself, (don't ask God to do it for you), under God's mighty hand, you enable Him to exalt you lift you up and honour you before men. Then in that exalted position, you give God the glory instead of taking the credit yourself. God's kingdom receives greater visibility and increase as a result of your light shining in the darkness of this world. "in due time" means don't get impatient with God. Your due season is approaching when it does not matter to you any more. You are content. You aren't disturbed or disquieted. You are thankful for God's blessings. You are content. You know God will exalt you in time, and you don't want it before then because you know you couldn't handle it anyway.

So how do you stop being self-centred? How do you come to the place of humility where your motive is no longer to serve your own interest but rather to exalt and magnify God and His kingdom?

Philippians 2:1-9

SO BY whatever [appeal to you there is in our mutual dwelling in Christ, by whatever] strengthening and consoling and encouraging [our relationship] in Him [affords], by whatever persuasive incentive there is in love, by whatever participation in the [Holy] Spirit [we share], and by whatever depth of affection and compassionate sympathy,

2 Fill up and complete my joy by living in harmony and being of the same mind and one in purpose, having the same love, being in full accord and of one harmonious mind and intention.

3 Do nothing from factional motives [through contentiousness, strife, selfishness, or for unworthy ends] or prompted by conceit and empty arrogance. Instead, in the true spirit of humility (lowliness of mind) let each regard the others as better than and superior to himself [thinking more highly of one another than you do of yourselves].

4 Let each of you esteem and look upon and be concerned for not [merely] his own interests, but also each for the interests of others.

5 Let this same attitude and purpose and [humble] mind be in you which was in Christ Jesus: [Let Him be your example in humility:]

6 Who, although being essentially one with God and in the form of God [possessing the fullness of the attributes which make God God], did not think this equality with God was a thing to be eagerly grasped or retained,

7 But stripped Himself [of all privileges and rightful dignity], so as to assume the guise of a servant (slave), in that He became like men and was born a human being.

8 And after He had appeared in human form, He abased and humbled Himself [still further] and carried His obedience to the extreme of death, even the death of the cross!

9 Therefore [because He stooped so low] God has highly exalted Him and has freely bestowed on Him the name that is above every name,

Check out the mind He had. He humbled himself and became obedient, and then God exalted Him. Humility produces obedience. When you are obedient to the word to the point that you die to self, God can highly exalt you . You will never be consistently obedient to the word of God unless you humble yourself.

What produces humility? Having the mind of a servant!

Mark 10:43-45

But this is not to be so among you; instead, whoever desires to be great among you must be your servant,

44 And whoever wishes to be most important and first in rank among you must be slave of all.

45 For even the Son of Man came not to have service rendered to Him, but to serve, and to give His life as a ransom for (instead of) many.

You can crucify the flesh, humble yourself, remove selfishness from your life and allow God to exalt you all through serving people.

How do I serve? By bringing others to Him and by supporting those who are involved in doing so. Make your resources available to your local church to reach out to others.

Serve your family. The more authority you have the more you should serve those who are accountable to you.

Feet washing(. John 13:4-8)

Got up from supper, took off His garments, and taking a [servant's] towel, He fastened it around His waist.

5 Then He poured water into the washbasin and began to wash the disciples' feet and to wipe them with the [servant's] towel with which He was girded.

6 When He came to Simon Peter, [Peter] said to Him, Lord, are my feet to be washed by You? [Is it for You to wash my feet?]

7 Jesus said to him, You do not understand now what I am doing, but you will understand later on.

8 Peter said to Him, You shall never wash my feet! Jesus answered him, Unless I wash you, you have no part with (in) Me [you have no share in companionship with Me].

Also John 13:15-17

For I have given you this as an example, so that you should do [in your turn] what I have done to you.

16 I assure you, most solemnly I tell you, A servant is not greater than his master, and no one who is sent is superior to the one who sent him.

17 If you know these things, blessed and happy and to be envied are you if you practice them [if you act accordingly and really do them].

Serving others will help close the door to pride and hence satan's deception.

Jesus is our example in serving. He served those who served Him. If you refuse to serve those who serve you, you have no part with Jesus. If you don't serve others, how will you ever close the door to pride?

Don't allow the demon of self to rule you any longer. To close the door to pride once and for all, deal with discontentment, become a thankful person and purpose in your heart to be a servant to others.

Do it by faith and say "Lord, I want to be able to serve from my heart. I want the very last remaining bit of pride removed from my life". You will see a miracle happen as the yoke of pride is supernaturally broken off of your life.

God bless.

LEADERSHIP IS INFLUENCE

In summary, Your personal development, undergoing the process of growth and maturity, embracing the Kingdom vision and all we have covered in this book are all designed to bring every reader to the place of conformity to Christlikeness in character and power. In living our lives to fulfill the purposes of God in all aspects of our lives. This is called fulfilling the destiny God has in store for us as individuals and corporately as the Church of the living God. Understanding the subject of leadership in God's kingdom will go a long way to help us rightly influence people around us, help us to be all we were called to be, and bring great pleasure to the heart of God our Father who sent His Son, our Lord Jesus Christ to pay the eternal price for our salvation. The summary of our understanding of leadership is captured in this chapter.

There are four C's involved in leadership in God's Kingdom.

1. The Call to leadership.
2. The Compassion of Christ.
3. The Connection with the people.
4. The Communication with the ones we are leading.

The call to Leadership.

It is vitally important for us to know that every believer is called to leadership. It is going through a process, cultivating our personal relationship with God as we recognise the potential He has invested in us and we respond to His call upon our lives. To influence others with the power and principles of His kingdom. We cannot give what we do not have. We may not all be called to lead big organisations but everyone is called to be a kingdom influence in their own world.

As we can see in Genesis 1:26-28 (AMPC)

26 God said, Let Us [Father, Son, and Holy Spirit] make mankind in Our image, after Our likeness, and let them have complete authority over the fish of the sea, the birds of the air, the [tame] beasts, and over all of the earth, and over everything that creeps upon the earth.

27 So God created man in His own image, in the image and likeness of God He created him; male and female He created them.

28 And God blessed them and said to them, Be fruitful, multiply, and fill the earth, and subdue it [using all its vast resources in the service of God and man]; and have dominion over the fish of the sea, the birds of the air, and over every living creature that moves upon the earth.

We were designed to have dominion(leadership). Men fell and lost the glory. But Christ came to restore the glory. He came to restore our dominion back to us.

Romans 3:23-26 (NKJV)

23 for all have sinned and fall short of the glory of God, 24 being justified freely by His grace through the redemption that is in Christ Jesus, 25 whom God set forth as a propitiation by His blood, through faith, to demonstrate His righteousness, because in His forbearance God had passed over the sins that were previously committed, 26 to demonstrate at the present time His righteousness, that He might be just and the justifier of the one who has faith in Jesus.

Hebrews 1:1-4 (KJV)

Hebrews 1:1 God, who at sundry times and in divers manners spake in time past unto the fathers by the prophets, 1:2 Hath in these last days spoken unto us by his Son, whom he hath appointed heir of all things, by whom also he made the worlds; 1:3 Who being the brightness of his glory, and the express image of his person, and upholding all things by the word of his power, when he had by himself purged our sins, sat down on the right hand of the Majesty on high; 1:4 Being made so much better than the angels, as he hath by inheritance obtained a more excellent name than they.

Romans 8:29-30 (NKJV)

29 For whom He foreknew, He also predestined to be conformed to the image of His Son, that He might be the firstborn among many brethren. 30 Moreover whom He predestined, these He also called; whom He called, these He also justified; and whom He justified, these He also glorified.

As we can see, everyone has leadership potential inside them. However, it doesn't translate to the influence God designed us to have in our lives over every other creation until this potential is discovered, developed and deployed. We are not to have dominion over other human beings. We are to have a positive influence where these are concerned.

When we think about the charge Jesus Christ gave to His disciples, we see He wants us to influence people for His kingdom with His love and power.

Mark 16:15-18 (NKJV)

15 And He said to them, "Go into all the world and preach the gospel to every creature. 16 He who believes and is baptized will be saved; but he who does not believe will be condemned. 17 And these signs will follow those who believe: In My name they will cast out demons; they will speak with new tongues; 18 they will take up serpents; and if they drink anything deadly, it will by no means hurt them; they will lay hands on the sick, and they will recover."

Matthew 28:18-20 (NKJV)

18 And Jesus came and spoke to them, saying, "All authority has been given to Me in heaven and on earth. 19 Go therefore and make disciples of all the nations, baptizing them in the name of the Father and of the Son and of the Holy Spirit, 20 teaching them to observe all things that I have commanded you; and lo, I am with you always, even to the end of the age." Amen.

The Compassion of Christ.

To lead as we are all created to do, it is of utmost importance we respond to this correctly.

To do it right, we need to have Compassion for people. Jesus clearly demonstrated His Compassion for people by many examples He showed us in the scripture.

When Jesus was moved with compassion we read how He healed the sick. His compassion is an expression of His love that releases His power to meet needs.

Mark 1:40-42 (NKJV)

Mark 1:40 And there came a leper to him, beseeching him, and kneeling down to him, and saying unto him, If thou wilt, thou canst make me clean. 1:41 And Jesus, moved with compassion, put forth his hand, and touched him, and saith unto him, I will; be thou clean. 1:42 And as soon as he had spoken, immediately the leprosy departed from him, and he was cleansed.

(Matt. 8:1–4; Luke 5:12–16)

40 Now a leper came to Him, imploring Him, kneeling down to Him and saying to Him, "If You are willing, You can make me clean."

41 Then Jesus, moved with compassion, stretched out His hand and touched him, and said to him, "I am willing; be cleansed." 42 As soon as He had spoken, immediately the leprosy left him, and he was cleansed.

Luke 7:13-15 (NKJV)

13 When the Lord saw her, He had compassion on her and said to her, "Do not weep." 14 Then He came and touched the open coffin, and those who carried him stood still. And He said, "Young man, I say to you, arise." 15 So he who was dead sat up and began to speak. And He presented him to his mother.

His love (the same love He showed as we can see in the scriptures above) is shed abroad in our hearts. So we can have His compassion for people.

Romans 5:5 (NKJV)

5 Now hope does not disappoint, because the love of God has been poured out in our hearts by the Holy Spirit who was given to us.

Called to be a Blessing:

There is a call to be a great blessing that manifests in our lives when embrace compassion for people in our leadership influence.

1 Peter 3:8-12 (NKJV)

8 Finally, all of you be of one mind, having compassion for one another; love as brothers, be tenderhearted, be courteous; 9 not returning evil for evil or reviling for reviling, but on the contrary, blessing, knowing that you were called to this, that you may inherit a blessing. 10 For "He who would love life And see good days, Let him refrain his tongue from evil, And his lips from speaking deceit. 11 Let him turn away from evil and do good; Let him seek peace and pursue it. 12 For the eyes of the LORD are on the righteous, And His ears are open to their prayers; But the face of the LORD is against those who do evil."

When we have Compassion for people, it helps people to discover God's will for their lives. We become the vessel in God's hand to influence people to do and become who and what God says they are.

The Connection with People.

To lead and lead effectively we need to Connect with people.

Connecting is the process where we identify with people, understand where they are in their walk of life and connect with them there. In Acts 3, Peter connected with the man at the gate beautifully. He needed some money from them but he gave him what money couldn't buy. Communication is effective when we connect with people. Connection with people is done by seeking something you have in common with them. It also involves inspiring and bringing them up to new levels in their walk with God.

Acts 3:4-8 (NKJV)

4 And fixing his eyes on him, with John, Peter said, "Look at us." 5 So he gave them his attention, expecting to receive something from them. 6 Then Peter said, "Silver and gold I do not have, but what I do have I give you: In the name of Jesus Christ of Nazareth, rise up and walk." 7 And he took him by the right hand and lifted him up, and immediately his feet and ankle bones received strength. 8 So he, leaping up, stood and walked and entered the temple with them—walking, leaping, and praising God.

Communication with the ones we are leading.

The place of effective communication is also important in our leadership.

Communication skills are effective when we know how to get our message across to the people.

The ability to transmit information to others in a way that they can appreciate and understand. Speaking in a way that honours others as well as seeking to encourage them to obey Godly principles.

SUMMARY

WE CAN SEE from the foregoing in this book that leadership is more about who you are, what you know and understand, what you can do and want to do as well as what capacity for leadership have you developed. Every part of our lives has potential to be developed as much as we want to develop. We need to know how to develop and commit to developing especially our leadership capacity. There is no end to development of our leadership capacity.

There is no end to our ability to add value to others.

As you study the materials covered in this book, over and over, realise that many things are written in a summarised version as individual development and application of the process and understanding is left to each person. In making decisions to stay humble, setting goals and walking in stewardship of everything around us. Each person emerges in the fullness of all that God has for them. They will have embraced kingdom vision as well as appreciate the need for personal development and being fully productive in life, they can go and manifest Christlikeness in all aspects of their lives.

There are three thoughts captured throughout the book, they are foundations, orientation and disposition. We need to lay a word-foundation for every aspect of our lives, our leadership development, as well our financial management, as well as our relationships. Jesus said if we build on sand, (human opinions), when the storms and winds blow, the house will fall and the fall will be great. The storms come not because we necessarily did anything wrong but it is one of the trials of living on earth. So let the Word of God be set as the basis for every thing we do. We do these things in honour of God and in obedience to His ways of doing things.

Orientation has to do with our willingness to grow, to develop and build our capacity in every aspect of life too. Growth must be intentional. Practices that make for growth must be committed to and practised regularly.

Our disposition is our attitude towards things and people in general. We need to have not just positive attitudes but correct ones based on the principles of God's word. For example, we understand that God is our Source even for material or financial provisions, then our jobs are channels. So we do not have a wrong disposition towards money or our jobs because we know our source.

Enjoy reading the book over and over and see how much God has invested in you to fulfil the potential inside you.

ABOUT THE AUTHOR

The Ministry of the
Rev. Michael Kola Ewuosho.

A long with his wife, he is the Co founder of the Fountain of Wisdom Ministries, an international Ministry with the vision to "Create a Forum where God's people can be equipped to flow with Him in wisdom and understanding. " . The purpose of the ministry includes enabling God's people to fulfil the purpose that He created them to fulfil. Together with his wife, they preach, teach and pray for people.

The Ministry has affected many nations since its inception and has installations in 5 different nations.

Websites include: www.fowm.org; www.kolaewuosho.com;

Rev. Michael Kola Ewuosho is the author of many books, including "Behind enemy lines" and "Understanding Leadership in God's Kingdom".

Many nations have been affected by the ministry, including many Latin American nations as well as nations in Asia. The nations include Costa Rica, Ecuador as well as Argentina amongst other nations . In Asia the nations include India and the Phillipines.

The emphasis has been the teaching the Word of God, then the right application and building people on the knowledge of the written Word of God, the bible, so they can grow into Christlikeness.

Church planting, raising leaders and itinerating have characterised this Ministry.

The goals include seeing many come to the Lord in their thousands, building up the Body of Christ in understanding and wisdom from the word of God, and then going on to disciple all nations according to the instructions from the Lord Jesus Christ.

His drive is to see people being built up to the fullness of God in Christ and help, inspire and equip people to fulfil the destiny that God has for them. God has great plans for His people. The more His people know about Him and His plans for them, the better they can participate with Him in the fulfilment of His purposes for their lives. Rev. Kola has a hunger to see this happen to many people.

www.ingramcontent.com/pod-product-compliance
Lightning Source LLC
Chambersburg PA
CBHW031226120626
46545CB00003B/1008